Movement

plus Rhymes, Songs, & Singing Games

Related Movement and Music Materials

Foundations in Elementary Education: Movement

Foundations in Elementary Education: Music

Foundations in Elementary Education: Music Recordings (cassettes, CDs)

Round the Circle: Key Experiences in Movement for Children

Movement Plus Music: Activities for Children Ages 3 to 7, Second Edition

Movement in Steady Beat

Teaching Folk Dance: Successful Steps

Cultures and Styling in Folk Dance

Rhythmically Moving 1–9 (records, cassettes, CDs)

Guide to Rhythmically Moving 1

Guide to Rhythmically Moving 2

Guide to Rhythmically Moving 3

Changing Directions 1–6 (records, cassettes, CDs)

Rhythmically Walking (cassettes)

Beginning Folk Dances Illustrated 1–6 (videos)

Teaching Folk Dance (video)

Available from
HIGH/SCOPE PRESS
600 North River Street, Ypsilanti, Michigan 48198-2898
ORDERS: phone (800) 40-PRESS, fax (800) 442-4FAX

Phyllis S. Weikart

Activities for Young Children

Movement

PLUS
Rhymes, Songs, & Singing Games

HIGH/SCOPE PRESS

a division of High/Scope Educational Research Foundation

Published by

HIGH/SCOPE PRESS

A Division of the
High/Scope Educational Research Foundation
600 North River Street
Ypsilanti, Michigan 48198-2898

(313) 485-2000, FAX (313) 485-0704

ISBN 1-57379-066-4

Printed in the United States of America

10 9 8 7 6

Contents

Preface   vii

How to Use This Booklet   1

Rhymes

Bubble Gum	6
Jack and Jill	7
Jack Be Nimble	8
Little Jack Horner	10
One, Two, Tie My Shoe	12
Ride a Fast Horse	13
Rub-a-Dub-Dub	14
Sally Go Round the Sun	16
Two Little Sausages	18
Wee Willie Winkie	19

Action Songs

Barnaclo Bill	22
The Beanbag Song	24
The Bears Climbed Up the Mountain	26
Beat Is Steady	28
Bluebird, Bluebird	30
Do As I'm Doing	32
Down Came a Bat	34
Down Came a Little Girl (Boy)	36
Eensy Weensy Spider	38
Everybody Pat With Jacob	40
The Farmer In the Dell	42
Follow, Follow	44
Goin' Round the Circle	46
Hokey Pokey	48
Jenny Mouse	52
Jumping Song	54
Jungle Beat	56
Let Everyone Move With Me	58
Little Green Frog	60
Little Red Wagon	62
Making Cookies	64

Old King Glory 66

Old Man Mosie 68

One In a Boat 70

Pizza Hut 72

Rock-a-Bye, Baby 76

Shake Our Bells 78

Shape Song 80

Someone Is the Leader 82

Start Your Day 84

Statue Shapes 86

Teddy Bear 88

Two Little Red Birds 90

Where Is Thumbkin? 92

Winter Time Is Here 94

Zach Pats His Knees 96

Preface

This revised booklet is designed as a supplement to three of the main program books: *Round the Circle: Key Experiences in Movement for Children; Foundations in Elementary Education: Movement;* and *Foundations in Elementary Education: Music.* It is one of the three activity booklets in the series; the other two booklets are titled *Movement Plus Music* and *Movement in Steady Beat.*

This booklet contains many of the rhymes and action songs originally published in the first edition of *Movement Plus Rhymes, Songs, & Singing Games.* Due to their continued popularity, these selections have been fully revised and expanded as appropriate for inclusion in this volume. In addition, I have selected four new action songs that open the door to even more opportunities for children to experience enjoyable movement and music activities. Another change in this edition is the elimination of the category "singing games." These activities are now included under the action-song category.

Rhymes and action songs introduce young children to a wide range of developmentally appropriate activities that reinforce and build movement abilities that are extremely important in the early years when the "body is the primary learning center." They are designed to be user-friendly and are easily presented to young children.

The original booklet was written with the assistance of seven endorsed trainers in the program I direct, "Education Through Movement: Building the Foundation." I am most grateful to trainers Jane Allman, Wyandotte, MI; Elizabeth B. Carlton, Salisbury, NC; Judith Cole, Corpus Christi, TX: Valerie Johnson, Olympia, WA; Penny Mahoney, Hadley, MA; Claudia Spring, Pontiac, MI; and Carol Kolonay-Spangler, Bridgeport, CT, for their help.

I would also like to extend my grateful appreciation and heartfelt thanks to Elizabeth (Libby) Carlton, endorsed trainer and author of the movement and music books, for the many hours of time she gave to the completion of this project. She created action songs that were added to this revised booklet, and she prepared all the songs for the computer-generated scores. In addition she added piano accompaniment for the *Movement Plus Rhymes and Action Songs: Recordings.*

Thanks also go to Jerry Bradshaw for the computer-generated musical scores and to Marcia LaBrenz, editor of the booklet.

I hope you will find this updated booklet to be a useful addition to your movement and music materials for young children.

How to Use This Booklet

he activities in this booklet are designed as a supplement to *Round the Circle: Key Experiences in Movement for Young Children; Foundations in Elementary Education: Movement;* and *Foundations in Elementary Education: Music.* All are available from High/Scope Press. The **key experiences in movement** addressed in this booklet are (1) Acting upon movement directions, (2) Describing movement, (3) Moving in nonlocomotor ways, (4) Moving in locomotor ways, (5) Moving with objects, (6) Expressing creativity in movement, (7) Feeling and expressing steady beat, and (8) Moving in sequences to a common beat. The **key experiences in music** include (1) Moving to music, (2) Exploring and identifying sounds, (3) Exploring the singing voice, and (4) Singing songs.

The activities are divided into two categories: (1) rhymes and (2) action songs. You will notice that many of the rhymes and action songs have been altered. These modifications are suggested to accommodate large groups of children and to allow more children to assume a leadership role and to problem solve and create. In some cases original language has been changed to make it more understandable for today's children.

The Learner SAY & DO sequence, when used consistently, helps children organize steady beat movements and movement sequences. Children speak words that define actions or body parts touched (SAY) and match the movement to the words (DO). The synchronization that occurs develops the cognitive-motor link to learning.

Organization of the Rhymes and Action Songs

Each activity is divided into the following components:

- *Title:* the title of the rhyme or song, along with the melody's original title where applicable.

- *Age:* the youngest age range for which the activity is generally appropriate.

- *Key Experiences:* a list of the major movement and music key experiences that the activity addresses.

- *Curriculum Concepts:* those ideas in the curriculum that can be addressed actively through the movement and music experiences. For example, the concepts "in and out" are reinforced in Verse 2 of the song *Hokey Pokey,* p. 48. Generally you will want to decide on the one concept that most clearly represents the reason you are using this activity with the children. Why is this activity introduced? What understanding do you hope the children will derive from this activity?

- *Description of the activity:* a brief overview of the activity.

- *Materials:* what equipment is needed and/or what song or rhyme you will need to familiarize yourself with in order to use the activity.

- *Activity to Experience:* the suggested lesson plan for introducing the activity. You may wish to insert other steps or leave out some depending on the ages of the learners. You will notice that every attempt has been made to let the children explore the concepts, to share their ideas with the class, and to be the leader for the activity. A number of the activities have children moving to the "macrobeat" or "microbeat," terms used by Dr. Edwin Gordon, a highly respected music learning theorist. The *macrobeat* in a rhyme or song is the first beat that organizes each group of two or three beats; each beat in the group is a *microbeat*. In addition, in many of the activities the teacher or leader uses an anchor word or anchor pitch to help children begin the activity with a common beat or pitch. The **anchor word** is a single word spoken by the leader four or eight times before saying a rhyme.

- *Facilitation and Reflection:* ways that you as the teacher might guide children to think, with suggested questions you might pose to the children. The exact wording of each question depends on the way in which the activity is experienced. You will notice that most of the questions do not have one correct answer. It is important to wait after asking the question to give children a chance to think and respond. Then you can facilitate and encourage several answers.

- *Extensions:* additional ideas for other ways to do the activity or to make it more appropriate for older or younger learners. Extensions also provide a way to do the activity at a future time.

Musical Score

The musical score is provided for each of the 36 action songs in this booklet. The song's title is given, followed by the range of pitches in the song. Songs with a range of 3 to 5 pitches are generally easier for preschool children to sing in tune. Also provided with each musical score are the **anchor pitches** for each song. The anchor pitch is the beginning pitch of a song sung by the leader using "Ready, let's sing" or "one, two, ready, sing," so all begin together on the same pitch. When the adult sings the anchor pitch or anchor pitches, children begin to sing in tune with the first pitch of the song. You will also notice that some words and/or syllables of words are underlined on the musical scores. These underlined words and syllables indicate the macrobeat, except where noted.

The Teaching Model

The recommended method for presenting the movement and music activities in this booklet incorporates the three components of the Teaching Model. These basic components are **separate, simplify,** and **facilitate.**

Separate. When presenting a movement or music activity use only one presentation modality at a time. In other words, **separate** the verbal directions from the demonstration and **separate** the verbal directions from any hands-on guidance (tactile assistance). Avoid describing while demonstrating, or demonstrating while describing. Also avoid giving verbal directions while you are assisting someone with hands-on guidance. For example, suppose you want to show putting the arms "in" for the first step of the *Hokey Pokey*. You might suggest that the children watch what your arms are going to do. You then move your arms in front of you without talking at the same time. Actions and verbal descriptions are kept separate. Children pay greater attention when **separate** is used.

Simplify. Movement tasks are made more manageable when they are broken down or simplified. To use the simplify technique with the *Hokey Pokey,* for example, put your arms "in" and then pause for the children to copy before putting your arms "out." In this way the sequence of two movements is simplified by making them two single movements that pause for a response before the second movement is shown. Take out the pause step when the children are comfortable performing the sequence. Another example of **simplify** is to present the movements for an action song before adding the words and the melody. Children then can participate even if they can't speak all the words or sing the song with all the pitches.

Facilitate. The **facilitate** component of the Teaching Model is designed to help children become active participants in the learning process by encouraging them to describe what they have experienced. Adults **facilitate** when they help children to develop an awareness of movement by combining their actions with thought and language. By asking appropriate questions, adults can encourage children to think rather than just to respond. The questions that provoke the most thought are divergent or open-ended ones that can have more than one correct answer and don't require a "yes" or "no" response.

Teaching Strategies

Adults should keep these general teaching suggestions in mind when selecting and presenting movement and music activities.

- Select activities at first that have only a few simple movements or leave out some of the less important movements in the beginning.

- At first, select rhymes and action songs in which children remain in their personal space or have only one child moving about the space rather than using activities that have all the children moving about the space. Space awareness takes time to develop in beginners of all ages.

- Encourage movement experiences in which children explore the concepts in their own ways and in their own timing. Remember that beginning movements should not require children to understand the directions "right" and "left" or to mirror the movements of the leader. These skills are more appropriate for older students (grade 2 and above) who have already tried the movement in their own way.

- Do the movements for a rhyme or song before adding the words and/or melody for that rhyme or song (or phrases of the rhyme or song).

- Encourage a child leader to set the tempo for the movement and then add the rhyme or song to the movement in that child's tempo. If the child leader begins in a tempo that is too slow or too fast for the other children, encourage that child to make the movements faster or slower.

- Pause in the rhyme or song at the ends of phrases to enable all the children to execute the movement or the sequence of movements.

Guidelines for Building the Child's Singing Foundation

The following general guidelines are designed to help adults develop and strengthen each child's basic singing foundation.

- Sing simple songs—ones that use the first two pitches that the child can sing in tune, such as G and E in the scale of C major (the 5–3 interval). These are the pitches sung in the phrase "Yoo-Hoo." Other simple pitches include those in the universal chant of childhood—"I'm going to tell on you" (5-3-6-5-3).

- Sing songs with pitches that tend to last longer, rather than short, fast pitches.

- Sing songs at a tempo appropriate for the beginner.

- Sing within the child's comfortable singing range. This range usually is higher than most adults prefer to sing.

- Sing songs that have repeated melodic patterns—the "Barney" song is a familiar example.

Recordings for the Action Songs

All of the songs in this booklet have been recorded on *Movement Plus Rhymes and Action Songs: Music Recordings.* The songs have been recorded to help you learn them, so *you* can sing them with the children. The **anchor pitch** or **anchor pitches** for each song are included also to help the adult with the first pitch of the song and in turn to help the children begin to sing with you from the very beginning of the song. Remember: It is very abstract for children to try to sing along with a recording when the recording artist isn't present.

Help get America singing again by joining the drive begun by the Music Educators' National Conference. Every young child needs to begin to develop a "personal song bank," and to add to that bank throughout the years in order to pass on this musical heritage to future generations.

Rhymes

Bubble Gum

Jack and Jill

Jack Be Nimble

Little Jack Horner

One, Two, Tie My Shoe

Ride a Fast Horse

Rub-a-Dub-Dub

Sally Go Round the Sun

Two Little Sausages

Wee Willie Winkie

Bubble Gum

Age 5-7

Key Experiences

- Moving in nonlocomotor ways
- Moving in locomotor ways
- Feeling and expressing steady beat

Curriculum Concepts

Combining speaking and moving

Steady beat

Number

Children keep the macrobeat while speaking the rhyme. A child chooses how many pieces of gum she wishes and what movement all should do while they count. The child leader freezes into a statue shape on the word "POP" and all copy.

Materials

Rhyme: *Bubble gum, bubble gum in a dish,*
How many pieces do you wish?
1, 2, 3. . . . POP!

Activity to Experience

Children learn the first two lines of the rhyme. They decide on a way to keep the macrobeat while they recite the rhyme. They also may wish to step in place to the microbeat as they speak the rhyme.

The teacher asks for a volunteer to decide on the number of pieces of gum he or she wishes (up to ten pieces). For example, Carol volunteers the number three and chooses a movement for all to do while they speak the rhyme.

Carol sets the beat for all to follow. The teacher speaks the **anchor word** "BEAT" four times, and all do Carol's movement while they speak the rhyme. As they count they also use Carol's selected movement. On POP Carol makes a statue shape and all copy.

Facilitation and Reflection

How were you keeping steady beat? How do you know the beat was steady?

What helped you combine speaking and moving?

Was it easy or hard to copy Carol's statue shape? What made it easy or hard?

Extensions

Younger children: The teacher counts to the number while the children do the movement.

All keep steady beat in their own ways.

Grade 2 and older students try jumping rope to the rhyme.

Jack and Jill

Age 3–5

Key Experiences

O—x Moving in locomotor ways

O—x Expressing creativity

Curriculum Concepts

Climbing

Falling

Children explore ways to climb a hill and then to fall down.

Materials

Mats to fall on

Rhyme: *Jack* and Jill went *up* the hill
To *fetch* a pail of *water.*
Jack fell down and *broke* his crown,
And *Jill* came tumbling *after.*

Activity to Experience

Children are encouraged to explore and talk about ways they might climb a hill. Children take turns being the leader and choosing a way to climb a hill; the other children copy the leader.

All the boys fall down as they think Jack might fall down. They may need to think about how to fall and not hurt themselves.

All the girls fall as they think Jill might do it.

Children act out the rhyme as the teacher and children who know the rhyme speak it. They climb in their own individual ways or copy the way one child suggests to climb.

Facilitation and Reflection

What are some ways we can climb up a hill?

What do we mean when we say we are climbing?

How did you fall?

What do we mean when we say we are falling?

Extensions

Have two children act out the rhyme and substitute their names for Jack and Jill. It doesn't have to be a boy and a girl.

Have the two children be the leaders and all climb and fall the way they do it. Divide the group in half.

Choose a different nursery rhyme that has actions and act it out.

Jack Be Nimble

Age 3–7

Key Experiences

- Moving in nonlocomotor ways
- Moving in locomotor ways
- Feeling and expressing steady beat

Curriculum Concepts

Combining speaking and moving

The concept of "over"

Taking off and landing (jumping)

Steady beat

Children explore jumping over their "candlesticks." They keep steady macrobeat while they speak the rhyme and then jump over at the end of the rhyme as they speak the word "JUMP."

Materials

Blocks or other objects (to represent candlesticks) that are easy to jump over

Rhyme: *Jack be nimble, Jack be quick.*

       Jack jump over the candlestick. JUMP!

Activity to Experience

Children explore jumping over their "candlesticks."

Children choose a place, such as their knees, to pat the macrobeat (the underlined words or syllables of the rhyme). The teacher brings the group together with the **anchor word** and then recites the rhyme while all keep beat.

Children jump over their "candlesticks" on the final word "JUMP."

Children are encouraged to speak the rhyme as they begin to learn it.

Facilitation and Reflection

How did you jump over your "candlestick"?

What does it mean to go over something?

What do we do when we jump?

Extensions

Change the rhyme to use the names of children who volunteer to show how they would go over the candlestick.

Change the words of the rhyme:

> *Jack* be nimble, *Jack* be quick.
>
> *Jack* go around the *candlestick*. WALK, WALK, WALK.

Tie a rope between two objects to be used as a "clothesline" for children to climb over or to crawl under.

> *Jack* be nimble, *Jack* be fine.
>
> *Jack* crawl under the *clothes*line.

Use this modification:

> *Jack* can wiggle, *Jack* can shake.
>
> *Jack* can show us a *statue* shape.

The child's name is used and all copy the child's statue.

Little Jack Horner

Age 3-5

Key Experiences

- Moving in nonlocomotor ways
- Expressing creativity

Curriculum Concepts

Combining speaking and moving

Body and space awareness terms

Children act out lines of the rhyme after exploring the concepts of "little," "eating," and "putting in and pulling out their thumb."

Materials

Rhyme: *Little Jack Horner <u>sat</u> in a corner,*
<u>Eat</u>ing a Christmas <u>pie.</u>
He <u>put</u> in his thumb, and <u>pulled</u> out a plum,
And <u>said,</u> "What a good boy am <u>I</u>!"

Activity to Experience

The teacher recites the first two lines of the rhyme; children explore making their bodies little and explore eating pie.

The adult recites the first two lines again, and the children act out the rhyme.

The teacher recites the third and fourth lines of the rhyme for the children to hear.

The teacher makes a fist with her thumb out and asks the children to copy. She turns the thumb down and up, and the children copy.

The last two lines of the rhyme are recited again, and the children act them out.

The adult again recites the entire rhyme, and all the children act out the sequence of movements.

Facilitation and Reflection

What did you do to make your body little?

What was Jack Horner doing when he was in the corner?

Why do you think he said he was a good boy?

Extensions

Children keep the macrobeat (the underlined words or syllables) while the teacher recites the rhyme.

One child acts out the rhyme; his or her name is used. The other children keep beat.

The children act out other nursery rhymes or action songs.

The children suggest other body parts to "put in and pull out" other than their thumbs. They also could suggest other foods to eat rather than "Christmas pie."

One, Two, Tie My Shoe

Age 4-7

Key Experiences

- ⚷ Moving with objects
- ⚷ Feeling and expressing steady beat
- ⚷ Moving in sequences to a common beat

Curriculum Concepts

Combining speaking and moving

Steady beat and sequencing

Children tap two different places with sticks in a sequence. They match the macrobeat of the rhyme with their tapping motions.

Materials

One pair of rhythm sticks, bobbins, or chopsticks for each child

Rhyme: <u>One,</u> two, <u>tie</u> my shoe;
<u>Three,</u> four, <u>shut</u> the door;
<u>Five,</u> six, <u>pick</u> up sticks;
<u>Seven,</u> eight, <u>lay</u> them straight;
<u>Nine,</u> ten, <u>start</u> again!

Activity to Experience

Children explore tapping their two sticks in different places both on and off the body. They use steady beat.

Children volunteer to be the leader for the class. All tap the place the leader chooses. The teacher adds learner SAY & DO with the tap, and all are encouraged to join in.

The teacher taps the floor one time and children copy. Then she taps her shoulders and children copy. This sequence is repeated slowly, and the words "FLOOR, SHOULDERS" are added.

After several repetitions of the pattern with learner SAY & DO, the rhyme is added, tapping on the underlined words of the rhyme.

A child suggests the next two places to tap. All try the pattern with learner SAY & DO, and the rhyme is repeated.

Facilitation and Reflection

Where did you tap your sticks? Was it easy or hard to tap the ends of the sticks? What made it easy? Hard?

What do we mean by tapping with a steady beat?

What is a sequence? Why is a sequence harder than tapping one place?

Extensions

Speak the rhyme using only a single place and not a sequence of two places.

Tap the sticks on paper plates placed upside down to create a drum.

Strike rhythm instruments on the macrobeat of the rhyme.

Ride a Fast Horse

Age 3-5

Key Experiences

- Moving in locomotor ways
- Expressing creativity

Curriculum Concepts

Representing

Wiggling

Children pretend to ride a horse. They wiggle fingers and toes and then act out the rhyme.

Materials

Rhyme: *Ride a fast horse to Banbury Cross,*

To see a fine lady upon a white horse;

Rings on her fingers and bells on her toes,

She shall have music wherever she goes.

Activity to Experience

Children are asked to pretend to ride on a horse and to talk about how they are doing it.

The teacher recites the first two lines of the rhyme while the children ride their horses.

The adult engages the children to wiggle their fingers and then to wiggle their toes inside their shoes. Then they wiggle their fingers and their toes at the same time.

The teacher sequences all the movements and adds the rhyme with the children acting out the lines. (It is important to recite the rhyme slowly enough and to pause at the ends of lines to give the children time to complete the movements.)

Facilitation and Reflection

How are you riding on your horse?

How did you make your fingers wiggle? Toes?

Extensions

Use broomsticks for riding the horses.

Put elastic bands with bells on them on each child's wrist and ankle.

Rub-a-Dub-Dub

Age 3–5

Key Experiences

- Moving in nonlocomotor ways
- Acting upon movement directions
- Expressing creativity

Curriculum Concepts

Body awareness

Washing

Children sit inside a hoop (a "bathtub") and show how they wash different parts of their bodies. They respond to the rhyme.

Materials

A hoop for each child

Rhyme (altered from the original):

> Rub-a-dub-dub, we sit in a tub,
> To give ourselves a bath.
> We wash our feet, we wash our legs,
> As we give ourselves a bath.

Activity to Experience

Children pretend they are sitting in the bathtub giving themselves a bath.

Children are asked what will be the first body part they wash. John suggests feet, and all wash their feet like John. Sally suggests legs next, and all watch Sally and do as she is doing.

The teacher recites the rhyme, and the children are encouraged to listen for the body part to wash. (Pause after feet and after legs to give the children time to pretend to wash.)

Repeat the rhyme again, and have the children choose other body parts to wash.

Facilitation and Reflection

How did you give yourself a bath?

What different parts of the body did we wash?

What does it mean to wash? What else can we wash besides our body?

Extensions

Alter the rhyme as follows: <u>Rub</u>-a-dub-dub, we get <u>out</u> of the tub,
    Be<u>cause</u> we have finished our <u>bath.</u>
    We <u>dry</u> our feet and we <u>dry</u> our legs,
    Be<u>cause</u> we have finished our <u>bath.</u>

Pretend to wash other things, such as windows, dishes, or the floor.

Sally Go Round the Sun

Age 3–7

Key Experiences

- Moving in locomotor ways
- Feeling and expressing steady beat
- Expressing creativity

Curriculum Concepts

The concept of "around"

Balance

Steady beat

Children walk to the beat, moving around the circle. The child leader moves around the inside of the circle. On the word "BOOM" the leader makes a statue shape that the others copy.

Materials

Rhyme: *Sally go a<u>round</u> the <u>sun.</u>*
        <u>Sal</u>ly go a<u>round</u> the <u>moon.</u>
        <u>Sal</u>ly go a<u>round</u> the <u>chim</u>ney <u>pot</u>
        <u>Eve</u>ry <u>af</u>ter<u>noon.</u> <u>BOOM!</u>

Note: The microbeat is underlined for walking.

Activity to Experience

Children walk around in a circle to a steady beat. The teacher speaks the **anchor word** "WALK, WALK, WALK, WALK" to match one child's walk and then recites the rhyme.

One child volunteers to be the leader and to walk inside the circle. That child's name is substituted in the rhyme. The child's walking tempo is used for the **anchor word.**

At the end of the rhyme, on BOOM, the child makes a statue shape that all copy.

A new child volunteers to be the leader.

Facilitation and Reflection

What do we mean when we say "go around"?

What else could we "go around"?

What does it mean to keep your balance in the statue?

Extensions

All of the children, except the leader, sit in a circle and keep beat. The leader goes around the inside of the circle on the rhyme and then makes the statue that all copy.

The children balance in their own statues on the word "BOOM."

Alter the rhyme, using the name of one of the children:

> _Eric_ go a_round_ the _table._ ___
> _Eric_ go a_round_ the _chair._ ___
> _Eric_ go a_round_ the _table,_ ___
> And _make_ a _statue_ there. ___

Two Little Sausages

Age 3–7

Key Experiences

- Moving with objects
- Feeling and expressing steady beat

Curriculum Concepts

Steady beat

Combining speaking and moving

Visual tracking

Children practice tapping their sticks on a paper plate. They respond to the word "BAM" in the rhyme by placing their sticks on some part of the body.

Materials

One paper plate and two sticks for each child. Chopsticks or drinking straws may be substituted.

Rhyme: <u>Two</u> little <u>sausages, Frying</u> in a <u>pan;</u>
   <u>One</u> went <u>POP; And the other</u> went <u>BAM!</u>

Activity to Experience

Children sit in an informal circle with the paper plate turned upside down in front of each child.

Each child has one pair of sticks (straws) and explores tapping the plate with the object. You may see children tapping with both sticks at the same time, with only one stick, or alternating sticks. On the word "BAM," each child decides where to freeze his or her sticks, such as on the shoulders, the knees, the head.

One child is the leader, setting a slower tempo. The teacher speaks the **anchor word** "TAP, TAP, TAP, TAP" to match the child leader's tempo and all tap together. The teacher then adds on the rhyme, synchronizing the tap with the underlined words or syllables of the macrobeat.

On the word "BAM" all freeze their sticks in the location each has chosen.

Facilitation and Reflection

How were you tapping your sticks?

Where did you freeze your sticks on the word "BAM"?

How did you know you were keeping steady beat?

Extensions

Children select two different places to freeze the sticks, one for the word "POP" and one for "BAM."

Children are given two plates so that two objects are struck at the same time, increasing the level of difficulty.

Children use hands against the body for the steady beat movement and some other movement for "BAM."

Wee Willie Winkie

Age 4–7

Key Experiences

- Moving in locomotor ways
- Expressing creativity

Curriculum Concepts

Representation

Combining speaking and moving

Children run in place while sitting or lying down; they run as if they are going upstairs and downstairs. They pretend to knock at a window and to call through a lock as in the rhyme, and then they pretend to sleep at the end.

Materials

Rhyme (modified): <u>Wee</u> <u>Willie</u> <u>Win</u> kie <u>runs</u> <u>through</u> the <u>town,</u> ___
      <u>Up</u> <u>stairs</u> and <u>down</u> <u>stairs</u> <u>in</u> his <u>night</u> <u>gown.</u> ___
      He <u>knocks</u> at the <u>win</u> <u>dow,</u>
      He <u>calls</u> <u>through</u> the <u>lock.</u>
      <u>Are</u> the <u>children</u> <u>in</u> their <u>beds?</u>
      It's <u>past</u> eight o'<u>clock!</u> ___

Activity to Experience

Children are seated in an informal circle. They are engaged in pretending that they are running. Some children may use their arms while others may lie on their backs and "run" with their legs.

The children pretend they are running upstairs and then downstairs.

Speak the first two lines of the rhyme, pausing after the words "town," "upstairs," and "downstairs." The underlined words and or syllables indicate the microbeat (the walking/running beat). Note that there is an additional microbeat after the words "town" and after "gown."

Speak the next two lines and ask the children how they would knock at a window and how they would call through a lock. You might wish to show the children a lock they could call through.

Speak the next two lines, and suggest the children represent how they would sleep in their beds.

Speak the entire rhyme, pausing for the children to represent the action words.

Facilitation and Reflection

What did you do to show you were running?

What did you do differently to show running upstairs? Downstairs?

If we knock on a window, how would we do it? Would it be a hard knock or a soft one?

When might you have to call through the lock on the door?

How do you sleep in your bed at home?

Extensions

Suggest to the children that they stand to run in place. Provide something to represent a window and a lock in order to represent those actions in the rhyme.

Have the children suggest other places to run and other things they could do and actions for those representations, thus changing the rhyme.

Action Songs

Barnacle Bill

The Beanbag Song

The Bears Climbed Up the Mountain

Beat Is Steady

Bluebird, Bluebird

Do As I'm Doing

Down Came a Bat

Down Came a Little Girl (Boy)

Eensy Weensy Spider

Everybody Pat With Jacob

The Farmer In the Dell

Follow, Follow

Goin' Round the Circle

Hokey Pokey

Jenny Mouse

Jumping Song

Jungle Beat

Let Everyone Move With Me

Little Green Frog

Little Red Wagon

Making Cookies

Old King Glory

Old Man Mosie

One In a Boat

Pizza Hut

Rock-a-Bye, Baby

Shake Our Bells

Shape Song

Someone Is the Leader

Start Your Day

Statue Shapes

Teddy Bear

Two Little Red Birds

Where Is Thumbkin?

Winter Time Is Here

Zach Pats His Knees

Barnacle Bill

Age 3–7

Key Experiences

- Moving in nonlocomotor ways
- Acting upon movement directions
- Feeling and expressing steady beat
- Moving to music

Curriculum Concepts

Steady beat

Rhyming words

Children respond to the parts of the body mentioned in the song by moving or patting in a steady beat. They listen to each verse of the song, patting in the macrobeat the part of the body or place mentioned in each verse.

Materials

Song: *Barnacle Bill*

Activity to Experience

The children pat a steady macrobeat together, one that the adult or one of the children initiates. As they pat steady beat, children should listen to the first verse of the song that the adult sings. As they listen, children discover the body part mentioned in the first verse (thumbs).

One child decides how everyone should keep beat with the thumbs.

Children can be encouraged to keep steady beat with the thumbs as the song is sung again.

They then listen for each new part of the body or place named in the other verses, keeping steady beat with each of the parts of the body or places.

Facilitation and Reflection

How were you keeping steady beat with your thumbs (on your shoes, etc.)? Have students recall.

Did you notice anything else about the song? (For example, the name of the body part rhymed with the number in each verse; each verse of the song was about Barnacle Bill; Barnacle Bill kept getting older in the song, etc.)

Extensions

Substitute names of children in the class for Barnacle Bill.

Challenge children who are age 5 and older to *find* something to pat that rhymes with the age of Barnacle Bill, rather than naming the item. For example, in the first verse, a child might beat a drum to rhyme with the word "one."

Suggest to the children that they might wish to change the words of the song to express something else about Barnacle Bill, such as "When Barnacle Bill was old . . . " or "When Barnacle Bill came home. . . ."

Barnacle Bill

(Range of 9 Pitches)

Traditional Tune

Verse 3: When Barnacle Bill was three,
       he learned to pat his knees . . .
       half past three.
Verse 4: When Barnacle Bill was four,
       he learned to pat the floor . . .
       half past four.
Verse 5: When Barnacle Bill was five,
       he learned to pat his thighs . . .
       half past five.

The Beanbag Song
(Jingle at the Window)

Age 4–7

Key Experiences

- Moving with objects
- Feeling and expressing steady beat
- Moving in sequences to a common beat
- Moving to music

Curriculum Concepts

Dropping

Passing (appropriate for children who are 6–7 years old)

Steady beat

Children are seated in a circle and drop a beanbag while the song is sung. Older students pass the beanbag.

Materials

One beanbag for each child in the circle

Song: *The Beanbag Song*

Activity to Experience

Children are seated close together in a circle. They hold a beanbag in one or both hands in front of themselves.

The teacher sings the first verse of the song and has the children listen for the word "drop." The song is sung again, and the children try to drop the beanbag as the word is sung. They pick up the beanbag after it is dropped so it can be dropped again.

Older students: Demonstrate to older children (generally ages 6 and 7) how to pass an *imaginary* beanbag in front to the next child to their right and how to bring their hands back in front of themselves.

Everyone speaks the word "PASS" and simultaneously passes the imaginary beanbag to the floor in front of the person on the right. They speak the words "PICK UP" and return their hands to the floor in front of themselves to pick up the imaginary beanbag that has been passed to them and wait to pass again.

Sing the song and have the children note when the word "pass" is sung. As the song is sung again pass the beanbag with the word "pass."

Now try passing the imaginary beanbags on the steady macrobeat of the song. Substitute the actual beanbag when all seem successful.

Use the same lead-up activities to pass to the left.

Facilitation and Reflection

How did you know when to drop (pass) the beanbag?

What does drop (pass) mean?

After you pass your beanbag, whose beanbag do you pass next?

Extensions

If children have been using two hands to pass the beanbag, they might try passing to the right with their right hand and to the left with their left hand.

Try substituting the words "TOSS" and "CATCH" for "DROP" and "PASS." Change the lyrics as follows:

> _Toss_ and catch it , _Ti_-de-o. _(3 times)_
>
> _Toss_ it up and catch it, _Ti_-de-o.
>
> _Ti_-de-o, _Ti_-de-o, _toss_ it up and catch it, _Ti_-de-o.

The Beanbag Song

(Range of 6 Pitches)

Traditional Tune

One and two, read-y, sing.

1. Drop the bean - bag, Ti - de - o. Drop the bean - bag, Ti - de - o.
2. Pass the bean - bag, Ti - de - o. Pass the bean - bag, Ti - de - o.

Drop the bean - bag, Ti - de - o, Drop it on the floor,____ Ti - de - o.
Pass the bean - bag, Ti - de - o, Pass it to the next one, Ti - de - o.

Ti - de - o, Ti - de - o, Drop it on the floor,____ Ti - de - o.
Ti - de - o, Ti - de - o, Pass it to the next one, Ti - de - o.

The Bears Climbed Up the Mountain
(The Bear Went Over the Mountain)

Age 3–7

Key Experiences

- Moving in locomotor ways
- Describing movement
- Expressing creativity
- Moving to music

Curriculum Concepts

The concept of "up"

Climbing

Children pretend they are moving like the bears in the song. They pretend to climb up the mountain. When they reach the top they look around.

Materials

Song: *The Bears Climbed Up the Mountain*

Activity to Experience

Children are encouraged to explore how bears in a zoo might move around.

They talk about how their bears are moving, and several children share with others.

The teacher asks, "Have any of you climbed up a mountain?" "What did you do, Tony, when you climbed the mountain?" "Let's pretend our bears are climbing up the mountain."

After the children begin, add the song.

Ask if any of the children heard the words "to see what they could see."

The children think about what they might see on top of the mountain. They pretend to look around.

At the end they hurry down the mountain.

Facilitation and Reflection

What did you have to do to climb the mountain?

How was it different when you pretended to be a bear?

What did you see from the top of the mountain?

Extensions

The children might think of other animals that could climb the mountain. Have them suggest a word that would describe the way the animal moved, such as the bird *flew* or the kangaroo *jumped*.

Encourage a child to choose a way for all to move and incorporate the movement in the song. For example, "Crawl up the mountain with Steven [3 times], and then we pat the beat. And then we pat the beat [2 times]. Crawl up the mountain with Steven [3 times], and then we pat the beat."

Children can think of other things to climb, like a slide, that can be incorporated in the song.

The Bears Climbed Up the Mountain

(Range of 6 Pitches)

Traditional Tune

One, two, sing with me.

The bears climbed up the moun - tain, the bears climbed up the

moun - tain, the bears climbed up the moun - tain to see what they could see. To

see what they could see. To see what they could see. The

bears climbed up the moun - tain, the bears climbed up the moun - tain, the

bears climbed up the moun - tain to see what they could see.

Beat Is Steady
(Are You Sleeping?)

Age 3–7

Key Experiences

- Moving in nonlocomotor ways
- Feeling and expressing steady beat
- Singing songs

Curriculum Concepts

Steady beat

Macrobeat (a term that can be used with 5–7-year-olds)

The concepts of "slow" and "fast"

Children pat a slow steady beat (macrobeat in the song) on their chest, following the teacher. As a common tempo is established, the song is sung. Different children suggest where to keep the beat and their name is inserted in the song.

Materials

Song: *Beat Is Steady*

Activity to Experience

The children are seated and the teacher begins to pat a slow beat on her chest. This tempo will be the macrobeat of the song. Children are encouraged to match the teacher's tempo on their chests. The teacher adds the **anchor word** "BEAT" spoken four times before beginning the song or sings the **anchor pitch** if the children will be singing.

One of the children suggests a new place to pat the macrobeat with both hands. For example, Andrew shows he is patting the floor. All join Andrew, the **anchor word** or **anchor pitch** is added, and the song is sung. The second and fourth lines of the song become "Andrew's beat, Andrew's beat." The underlined words or syllables of the song represent the macrobeat.

You might wish to try a rocking beat with all the children in the circle close together.

Facilitation and Reflection

How did you know when to pat the beat?

What were the different places we used for patting the slow beat?

Which children were the leader? Where did they pat?

Extensions

Children suggest using teddy bears, other stuffed animals, or dolls to keep the beat and to rock with.

Two children can sit inside a Hula-Hoop and rock together in "row, row, row your boat" style.

Two children can hold sticks together and keep the beat. Keep the tempo of the song slow enough to allow the response on the beat.

Verse 2 of the song may be added for children who are 5–7 years old.

Beat Is Steady

(Range of 9 Pitches)

Adapted
French Folk Song

One, two, sing with me.

1. Beat is stea - dy, beat is stea - dy,
2. Keep the mac - ro, keep the mac - ro,

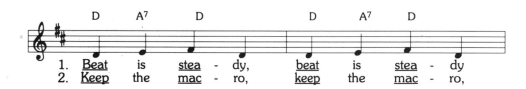

Feel the beat, feel the beat.
Or-gan - i-zing beat, or-gan - i-zing beat.

Keep the beat so stea - dy, keep the beat so stea - dy.
Mac - ro-beats have ac - cents, mac - ro-beats have ac - cents,

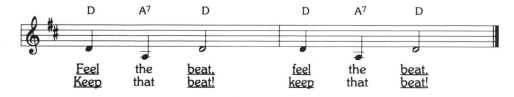

Feel the beat, feel the beat.
Keep that beat! keep that beat!

Bluebird, Bluebird

Age 4–7

Key Experiences

- Moving in nonlocomotor ways
- Moving in locomotor ways
- Feeling and expressing steady beat
- Moving to music

Curriculum Concepts

Steady beat

The concept of "through"

Children walk through "windows" made by half of the group while the first verse of the song is sung. On the chorus of the song, they find a friend and pat each other on the shoulder using the steady macrobeat.

Materials

Song: *Bluebird, Bluebird*

Activity to Experience

Encourage some of the children to make windows by joining hands and raising their arms. The children not joined in windows decide how they wish to fly through the windows without bumping other children. The first verse of the song is sung.

The two groups of children change roles. Those who made the windows before now fly through them, and vice versa. The second verse of the song is sung.

Suggest to the children that they find one friend and pat each other on the shoulders using both hands. As the teacher speaks the **anchor word** "PAT," all synchronize their pats. The chorus of the song is sung while the children keep the macrobeat.

The song is sung again with children deciding what color birds they wish to be. They also decide where they wish to pat another friend and that body part is substituted in the song's chorus.

The teacher adds the **anchor pitch** when the children are ready to join in singing.

Facilitation and Reflection

What were the birds doing as the song was sung?

How did you fly through the windows? What does the word *through* mean? What else do we go *through*?

How did you know you were patting steady beat?

Extensions

Change from birds to other animals, such as dogs, and have children represent dogs crawling through the windows.

Change the theme of going through windows to going around the table or through the doorway.

Sing the song at transition times in the preschool and change the words accordingly. For example,

> *Clean* up, *clean* up, *time* for *clean* up. (3x)
>
> *Put* all your *work* time *things* away.

Chorus: *Take the blocks, put* them on the *shelves now.* (3x)

> *Put* all your *blocks* away now.

Bluebird, Bluebird

(Range of 6 Pitches)

Adapted Folk Song

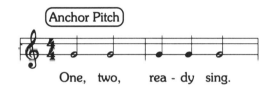

One, two, rea - dy sing.

1. Blue -bird, blue -bird, thru my win -dow. Blue -bird, blue -bird, thru my win - dow.
2. Red - bird, red -bird, thru my win -dow. Red - bird, red -bird, thru my win - dow.

Blue - bird, blue - bird, thru my win - dow. Keep sing - ing and be hap - py.
Red - bird, red - bird, thru my win - dow. Keep sing - ing and be hap - py.

Chorus

Find a friend, pat 'em on the shoul- der. Find a friend, pat 'em on the shoul- der.

Find a friend, pat 'em on the shoul- der. Keep sing - ing and be hap - py.

Do As I'm Doing

Age 4–7

Key Experiences

- Moving in nonlocomotor ways
- Feeling and expressing steady beat
- Moving to music
- Singing songs

Curriculum Concepts

Steady beat

Anchored movement

Children explore movements they can do while anchored (sitting, lying down, standing). One child is the leader and the others copy. The song is added to the child's beat, and all sing that child's name in place of "me."

Materials

Carpet squares

Song: *Do As I'm Doing*

Activity to Experience

Encourage children to explore nonlocomotor movements that they can do while anchored on their carpet squares. Such movements might include shaking, pounding, twisting, and swinging.

Ask for a volunteer to do a movement for everyone to copy. As the children copy the leader's movements encourage them to talk about what the leader is doing.

The teacher begins his movement slowly with a steady beat; then he speaks the **anchor word** to help everyone match the steady beat ("POUND, POUND, POUND, POUND") and sings the song.

Greg volunteers to be the next leader and all copy. If children are encouraged to join in the song, the teacher begins with the **anchor pitch** of the song.

Facilitation and Reflection

What movements can you do when you are anchored on your carpet square?

What did Greg do in his twisting movement?

What does it mean to move in steady beat?

Extensions

Older children (ages 5–7) might work in pairs with one Hula-Hoop for each pair. The person in the hoop is the leader, and the person outside the hoop is the follower. Each time the song ends, have the copier describe the movement copied.

Use locomotor movements instead of nonlocomotor movements.

Do As I'm Doing

(Range of 8 Pitches)

Traditional Tune

One, two, read - y, sing.

Do as I'm do - ing, fol - low, fol - low me!

Do as I'm do - ing, fol - low, fol - low me!

If I do it high or low, If I do it fast or slow,

Do as I'm do - ing, fol - low, fol - low me!

Do as I'm do - ing, fol - low, fol - low me!

Down Came a Bat
(Down Came a Lady)

Age 4–7

Key Experiences

- Moving in nonlocomotor ways
- Moving in locomotor ways
- Expressing creativity
- Moving to music
- Exploring the singing voice

Curriculum Concepts

Space awareness

The concepts of "up" and "down"

Higher and lower pitches

Children talk about bats and how they fly. They move about the space using their "radar" so as not to fly into anyone's space. During the interlude of the song they use vocal exploration.

Materials

Song: *Down Came a Bat*

Activity to Experience

The teacher shows the children a picture of a bat and asks if anyone has ever seen a bat. She then sings the song and asks the children what the bats do at the end of the song.

Since bats fly, the children explore arm movements that might represent the wings of the bat.

Encourage the children to talk about their movements.

Tell the children that bats use a special kind of radar when they fly around so they don't fly into anything or anybody. The children are encouraged to put on their "radar" and to fly about the space, moving down low and up high, without touching anyone else. They use vocal sounds while they fly.

After the children are comfortable moving about the space, add the song.

Add vocal exploration with movement at the end of the song.

Facilitation and Reflection

How are you moving your arms to fly like a bat?

What did you have to do to keep from flying into anyone else?

How did you make your bat go up and down?

What did you do with your body when your voice went higher and lower?

Extensions

Think about other things that fly, such as birds, butterflies, or airplanes, and substitute them in the song.

Read a story to the children that tells about something flying and have the children represent the flying.

Down Came a Bat

(Range of 3 Pitches)

Traditional Tune

EXTENSIONS:
Add vocal exploration and purposeful movement for other musical concepts, such as loud-soft, smooth-staccato, etc.

Down Came a Little Girl (Boy)

(Down Came a Lady)

Age 3–7

Key Experiences

- Moving in nonlocomotor ways
- Expressing creativity
- Feeling and expressing steady beat
- Moving to music

Curriculum Concepts

Moving in different types of shoes

Taking off and landing

Children perform locomotor movements in their jumping shoes or other types of shoes while listening to the song.

Materials

Song: *Down Came a Little Girl (Boy)*

Activity to Experience

Children explore different ways to jump in their jumping shoes. One child becomes the leader and shares her way to jump, while the rest of the class copies. Then another child also is the leader. All talk about the leaders' ways to jump. The teacher speaks the **anchor word** "JUMP" to the leader's beat, or sings the **anchor pitch** if children are also singing, and the song is sung. The two leaders are jumping about the space, while the others jump in their personal space.

Other children share their way to jump and the song is repeated.

Children then are encouraged to explore what they can do in other types of "movement shoes," such as marching, hopping, and jogging.

Sing the second verse with two boys as the leaders in their marching shoes. Note that the microbeat is underlined for the marching.

Facilitation and Reflection

What special way did you take off and land in your jumping shoes?

What other kinds of shoes did you try?

What shoes were the easiest to move in? The hardest?

Extensions

Substitute the children's names in the song.

Have children think of other types of shoes, such as ballet shoes, mommy or daddy shoes, or cowboy boots.

Down Came a Little Girl (Boy)

(Range of 3 Pitches)

Traditional Tune

One, two, sing with me.

Down came a lit - tle girl, down came two.

Down came lit - tle girls, in their jump - ing shoes.

Jump, jump, jump, jump, jump and stop!

* Down came a lit - tle boy, down came two.

Down came lit - tle boys, in their march - ing shoes.

March, march, march, march, march, march, stop!

* In this verse, the microbeat is underlined to concur with the marching beat.

Eensy Weensy Spider

Age 3–7

Key Experiences

- Moving in nonlocomotor ways
- Moving in sequences to a common beat
- Moving to music
- Singing songs

Curriculum Concepts

The concepts of "up" and "down"

Children experience simplified movements for this action song. After each action is copied the part of the song for that action is added.

Materials

Song: *Eensy Weensy Spider*

Activity to Experience

Children watch and copy the teacher's motions of wiggling the fingers of both hands as the arms are raised up in front of the body. The children talk about what the wiggling fingers might represent. The teacher adds on the first phrase of the song and asks the children what the wiggling fingers represented.

The second movement is added, that of pointing the fingers toward the floor and moving the arms down without wiggling the fingers. The children are asked what was different as the arms came down compared to when they went up.

The two motions are sequenced, followed by the song's first two phrases. There is no movement added for "washed the spider out."

Children are encouraged to make their arms look like the shape of the sun, and the third phrase of the song is added (no movement for "dried up all the rain").

The teacher sings the last phrase and asks the children to recall how the spider climbed up.

The song with all the motions is repeated. If the children are singing, begin with the **anchor pitch.**

Facilitation and Reflection

What was different about the fingers when the arms came down compared to when they went up?

How did you show the shape of the sun?

How could you make the spider go up in a different way? How could you make the rain come down in a different way?

At what other times might we use "up" and "down" (on a slide, on the stairs, while climbing a tree)?

Extensions

Add the children's ideas for motions to accompany "wash the spider out" and "dried up all the rain."

Think of other creatures or animals that could climb up and things that could come down. Write new words for the song.

Read *Itsy Bitsy Spider* by Iza Trapani and act out the six verses.

Eensy Weensy Spider

(Range of 8 Pitches)

Traditional Tune

One, two, read-y, sing.

Een - sy ween - sy spi - der went up the wat - er spout.

Down came the rain and washed the spi - der out.

Out came the sun and dried up all the rain, and the

Een - sy ween - sy spi - der went up the spout a - gain.

Everybody Pat With Jacob
(Mary Had a Little Lamb)

Age 3–7

Key Experiences

- ○─ᴎ Moving in nonlocomotor ways
- ○─ᴎ Feeling and expressing steady beat
- ○─ᴎ Moving to music
- ○─ᴎ Singing songs

Curriculum Concepts

Steady beat

Body awareness

Nonlocomotor movements (appropriate for children who are 5 and older)

Children explore patting steady beat with both hands on different parts of the body. One child is the leader and all copy that child. The song is added to the leader's beat.

Materials

Song: *Everybody Pat With Jacob*

Activity to Experience

Children are seated in an informal circle. They are encouraged to find various places on their bodies where they can softly pat steady beat with two hands (spider pats).

Ask for a volunteer to be the leader. Jacob volunteers to be the leader. All the children copy Jacob's movement and his steady beat.

Before singing the song, speak the **anchor word** "PAT"—or the name of the body part—four times, and layer on the song to the established beat. When the children know the song, replace the **anchor word** with the **anchor pitch,** so all can sing together from the song's first pitch.

Facilitation and Reflection

What different places did you pat steady beat when you were exploring?

What places did we pat as we sang the song?

What does it mean to keep steady beat?

Extensions

Encourage the children to try other movements, such as shaking, pounding, or twisting. Also try locomotor movements in steady beat, such as marching, jumping, or galloping.

See *Zach Pats His Knees* (page 96), sung to the tune of *Jimmy Crack Corn,* and substitute the new words. Have the children "freeze" on the word "stop."

Everybody Pat With Jacob

(Range of 5 Pitches)

Traditional Tune

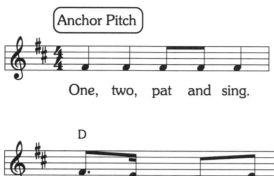

One, two, pat and sing.

1. Ev - 'ry - bod - y pat with Ja - cob,
2. Ev - 'ry - bod - y pat with Phyl - lis,

pat with Ja - cob, pat with Ja - cob.
pat with Phyl - lis, pat with Phyl - lis

Ev - 'ry - bod - y pat with Ja - cob.
Ev - 'ry - bod - y pat with Phyl - lis.

Who is our next lead - er?
Now our game is o - ver!

The Farmer In the Dell

Age 5–7

Key Experiences

- Moving in locomotor ways
- Expressing creativity
- Feeling and expressing steady beat
- Moving to music

Curriculum Concepts

Steady beat

Space awareness

Children are in groups of five; one child in each group chooses one of the characters in the song. They decide how they are going to move when it is their turn. The singing game is performed.

Materials

Song: *The Farmer In the Dell*

Activity to Experience

Children are in groups of five. Each child in the group chooses one of the characters in the song. Each child decides how his or her chosen person would move. For example, how would the farmer, the wife, or the child move?

Have all the "farmers" show how they are going to move about the space in steady beat. Repeat with the other characters in the song. The children don't need to join hands as in the original singing game. They finally are moving about the space one behind the other in their lines of five, but all are moving differently.

Sing the song and perform the movements.

Facilitation and Reflection

How do you think a farmer would move? [A wife, child, etc.?]

What did you do to make your movement like a farmer? [A wife, child, etc.?]

How did you keep from bumping into the other groups?

Extensions

Each character after the farmer might teach his or her way of moving to the others. For example, the wife teaches her move to the farmer, the child teaches to the wife and farmer, etc. At the end all are moving like the dog mentioned in the last verse of the song, and all are joined together.

Each group of five might make a group statue shape at the end of the song. The statue then tries to move.

The Farmer In the Dell

(Range of 9 Pitches)

Children's Play Song

1. The farm - er in the dell. The farm - er in the dell.
2. The farm - er takes a wife. The farm - er takes a wife.

Hi! Ho! The der - ry o! The farm - er in the dell.
Hi! Ho! The der - ry o! The farm - er takes a wife.

Verse 3: The wife takes a child.
The wife takes a child.
Hi! Ho! The derry-o!
The wife takes a child.

Verse 4: The child takes a nurse.
The child takes a nurse.
Hi! Ho! The derry-o!
The child takes a nurse.

Verse 5: The nurse takes a dog.
The nurse takes a dog.
Hi! Ho! The derry-o!
The nurse takes a dog.

Create other verses as desired.

Follow, Follow
(Adapted from *Hey, Lidee Lidee*)

Age 3–7

Key Experiences
- Moving in nonlocomotor ways
- Moving in locomotor ways
- Expressing creativity
- Feeling and expressing steady beat
- Moving to music

Curriculum Concepts

The concept of "following"

Steady beat

Musical patterns

Children choose movements to do in steady beat. Several children become leaders and all follow. The song is sung.

Materials

Song: *Follow, Follow*

Activity to Experience

Karen, the adult in the classroom, sings the song while keeping steady beat in front of her on the floor. The children are encouraged to copy Karen's steady beat.

Children explore ways to keep steady beat in either nonlocomotor or locomotor ways. Matthew shares his steady beat of shaking both hands in front of his body. The others copy, and Karen speaks the **anchor word** "SHAKE" 4 times and then adds the song with Matthew's name in it. If the children are going to sing with her, she begins with the **anchor pitch** of the song.

Other children become the leader, and their names are added in the song.

Facilitation and Reflection

What does it mean to follow a leader?

How did I keep steady beat? How did Matthew keep steady beat?

Are there other times you might be asked to follow a leader?

Extensions

The song also can be used as a transition time song. For example, sing "Now it's snack time . . ." or "Now we clean up . . ."

Use the song for statue shapes

Older children (age 5 and older) might choose sequences of movement for the class to follow. For example, a child might bend, straighten, or tap his knees, then his shoulders.

Follow, Follow

(Range of 5 Pitches)

Adapted Folk Song

Anchor Pitch

One, two, sing with me.

C   C

1. Fol - low, fol - low, fol - low Ka - ren.
2. Fol - low, fol - low, fol - low Mat - thew.

C   G⁷

— She is the lead - er _____ now!
— He is the lead - er _____ now!

G⁷   G⁷

Fol - low, fol - low, fol - low Ka - ren.
Fol - low, fol - low, fol - low Mat - thew.

G⁷   G⁷   C

— She is the lead - er _____ now!
— He is the lead - er _____ now!

Verse 3: Now it's snack time. Now it's snack time.
                  Get ready, find your place.
                  Now it's snack time. Now it's snack time.
                  Get ready, find your place.

Goin' Round the Circle (Go Tell Aunt Rhody)

Age 5–7

Key Experiences

- Moving in nonlocomotor ways
- Moving in locomotor ways
- Expressing creativity
- Moving to music
- Singing songs

Curriculum Concepts

Steady beat

The concept of "around"

Children are marching around the circle with a partner, and the song is sung. Another child volunteers to skate, and all copy that movement.

Materials

Song: *Goin' Round the Circle*

Activity to Experience

Children, in pairs, are standing in a circle in order to go around all the tables in the room. The teacher asks, "Who would like to plan a way to travel around the circle. Mike, how are you and Ben going to travel around the circle?"

Mike and Ben choose marching, and all go around the circle to their marching beat. The teacher adds the **anchor word** "MARCH" spoken 4 or 8 times depending on the tempo of march. If the children are going to sing the song, the **anchor pitch** is sung to set the first note of the song and the tempo of the walk. *Note:* In the song the macrobeat is underlined, but the leader may use a microbeat tempo.

Children each choose another friend and decide on a different way to travel. Elisa and Heather choose skating and all copy. The **anchor word** or **anchor pitch** is added and the song is sung.

Facilitation and Reflection

What do we mean when we say travel *around* the circle?

How did Mike and Ben travel around? (Elisa and Heather?)

What other ways of traveling around did you think about?

Extensions

All the children might sit in a circle and rock to the steady beat. One child volunteers to go around the outside of the circle. The words of the song can be changed to use the child's name, such as "Mike marches 'round the circle." The action Elisa has chosen may be incorporated, such as "Skate around the circle."

Have all the children choose a way to travel around the circle and sing the song.

Have all the children sit in the circle and sing "Rocking in the circle."

Goin' Round The Circle

(Range of 5 Pitches)

Traditional Tune

One, two, ready, sing.

Go - in' round the cir - cle,

Go - in' round the cir - cle.

Go - in' round the cir - cle and

now we need a new friend.

Hokey Pokey

Age 3–7

Key Experiences

- ⊶ Moving in nonlocomotor ways
- ⊶ Moving in locomotor ways
- ⊶ Feeling and expressing steady beat
- ⊶ Moving in sequences to a common beat
- ⊶ Moving to music

Curriculum Concepts

In and out

Up and down

Turning around

Children learn the parts of this action song cumulatively. The specific action or actions in the song are learned first, and then after these actions are processed by the children either verbally or visually, the lines of the song corresponding to the actions are added.

Materials

Song: *Hokey Pokey*

Activity to Experience

Children copy the adult's static motion of putting both arms straight in front of the body (into the circle). Then they copy the static motion of putting the arms out behind them (out of the circle).

The children sequence the two motions. The first line of the song is sung, and children join with the motions. (If the children are young, you might wish to pause in the song after the "in" and also after "out.")

Continue with verbal directions, or with a visual demonstration for the arms to go "in" again, followed by a shaking motion of both arms.

Encourage the children to do all four motions.

Sing the first two lines of the song with the children doing the motion. Pause slightly after each movement so the children are successful.

With verbal directions, suggest that the children find a funny way to turn all the way around.

Have them talk about their funny way. Add the three lines of the song.

Demonstrate a patting of the legs—four slow pats in steady beat. After the children have done it with you, sing the last line of the song with a "Hey" on the end. Notice the use of movement with 4 steady beats rather than movement to the rhythm of the words.

Sing the entire song while the children do the movements.

Have the children explore other parts of the body that could be moved in and out, such as one leg or the head. Use the ideas the children generate and sing the song again.

Facilitation and Reflection

Where did the arms go first? Second?

What did you do to move in a funny way as you turned around?

What does it mean to put your arms "in" and "out"?

Extensions

Use concepts of up and down and turning the arms around and around, and sing the second verse of the song. Note the use of the static pause on the recording.

Use a stuffed animal or doll and move the doll or animal's arms with the song.

Change the words to represent special occasions during the year, such as "Do the turkey trot all the way around" in November or "Do the Hooky Spooky and you turn yourself about, Now everybody shout BOO!" for Halloween or "Roll your body with an Easter egg roll."

Hokey Pokey

(Range of 6 Pitches)

Adapted Folk Song

One, two, sing.

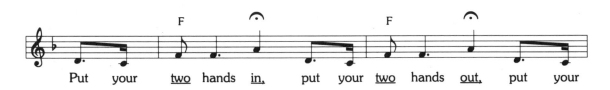

Put your two hands in, put your two hands out, put your

two hands in and shake them all a - bout. You

do the hok - ey pok - ey and you turn your - self a - round.

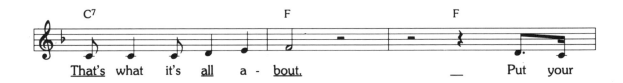

That's what it's all a - bout. ___ Put your

two   hands   **up,**   put   your   two   hands   down,   put   your

two   hands   up   and   then   you   put   them   down.   You

turn   both   arms   a - round   and   a - round.   A -

round   and   a - round.   A - round   and   a - round.

Pat   your   knees   and   "boom"   the   ground.   BOOM!

Jenny Mouse
(Paw Paw Patch)

Age 3-7

Key Experiences

- Moving in nonlocomotor ways
- Moving in locomotor ways
- Expressing creativity
- Feeling and expressing steady beat
- Moving to music

Curriculum Concepts

The concept of "around"

Steady beat

Children are seated and performing a movement in steady beat while one volunteer plans a way to go around the circle while the song is sung.

Materials

Song: *Jenny Mouse*

Activity to Experience

Encourage the children to find a way to keep steady beat while the teacher sings the song.

Ask several children to share their way to keep steady beat. All try the leader's movement.

Ask for a volunteer to plan a way to travel around the circle. Jenny volunteers.

As Jenny walks around the circle, the other children follow one leader with her beat-keeping movement to the song.

When singing the song insert the name of the child who is going around the circle in place of "Jenny." You can also insert the chosen action, such as "Allison Mouse, jog around the circle."

Facilitation and Reflection

What movement did you do in steady beat while the song was sung?

What does it mean to go around the circle?

What did Jenny do as she went around the circle? What did Allison do?

Extensions

All the children make a plan for a way to go around the circle at the same time. You might use "Children Mice go around the circle."

Substitute a different animal for mice.

School-aged children could work with a partner; one person makes a plan for going around the circle while the other person makes a plan for keeping steady beat. One partner might tell the other how to keep steady beat, while the other tells how to travel around. See also *Goin' Round the Circle* on p. 46.

Jenny Mouse

(Range of 8 Pitches)

Traditional Tune

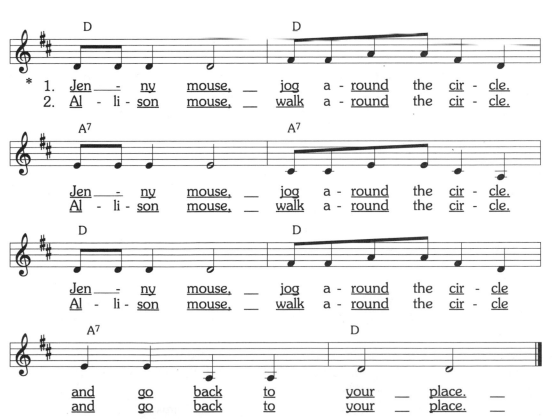

*1. Jen - ny mouse, __ jog a - round the cir - cle.
2. Al - li - son mouse, __ walk a - round the cir - cle.

Jen - ny mouse, __ jog a - round the cir - cle.
Al - li - son mouse, __ walk a - round the cir - cle.

Jen - ny mouse, __ jog a - round the cir - cle
Al - li - son mouse, __ walk a - round the cir - cle

and go back to your __ place. __
and go back to your __ place. __

* In this song, the microbeat (for jog and walk) is underlined.

Jumping Song
(Here We Go Round the Mulberry Bush)

Age 4–7

Key Experiences

- Moving in locomotor ways
- Expressing creativity
- Feeling and expressing steady beat
- Moving to music

Curriculum Concepts

Taking off and landing

Steady beat

Children explore different ways to jump, and then share their ideas with others. As a child performs the motions, the song is sung.

Materials

Song: *Jumping Song*

Activitiy to Experience

Children are encouraged to spread out about the space.

They explore jumping in different ways. Children volunteer to share their way of jumping, and the others copy and talk about it. The song is sung as all the children jump in Gretchen's way. Other children become the leader and the first verse of the song is repeated.

The children are asked to think of other movements they might do to the song. They try out and talk about the suggestions that can be incorporated into the song, such as "Nathan gallops."

Facilitation and Reflection

What was special about Gretchen's way of jumping?

How do we take off and land when we are jumping?

What other movement did you try?

Extensions

Change the action and the words, such as "This is the way we swing on the swing, or ride the bike, or climb the ladder."

Children think about a time of the year, such as Easter time, and what special events might happen on Easter, such as gathering eggs or coloring eggs or going to church. These ideas are explored with movement and are added to the song.

Use animals and actions associated with them, such as "horses trot," "birds fly," and "elephants walk."

Jumping Song

(Range of 8 Pitches)

Traditional Tune

Jungle Beat

Age 4–7

Key Experiences

- Moving with objects
- Expressing creativity
- Feeling and expressing steady beat
- Exploring and identifying sounds

Curriculum Concepts

Steady beat

Tapping

Sound exploration

Children explore the various steady beat sounds that they can make with their sticks as they tap different body parts, tap the floor, and hit or rub the sticks together. One child is the leader for the movement as the song is sung.

Materials

One pair of sticks for each child

Song: *Jungle Beat*

Activity to Experience

Children first explore sounds they can make with the sticks. They share their way of making sounds and describe the sounds.

Working singly or in pairs, children match each other's steady beat; an individual or pair leads the class.

One person begins the steady beat sound; the teacher speaks an **anchor word** and then sings the song using the beat established by the leader. All the children use the movement of the leader(s).

Another person or pair becomes the leader and the song is sung to that beat. When the children can sing the song, begin with the **anchor pitch** as sung on the recording.

Facilitation and Reflection

What did Greg's sound remind you of? Natasha's sound?

What did Greg do with his sticks to make his sound? What did Natasha do with her sticks?

What did you do to copy the steady beat?

Extensions

Younger children might pat the beat on a stuffed animal or doll.

Older children: Change the pairs to groups of three or four children. Change the song to reflect the number in each group. At the end of the song children count to that number as they tap the floor.

Use a single child as the leader and sing that child's name. The song becomes "Kevin monkey cool and neat . . ."

Substitute the hands to make sounds or use rhythm instruments in steady beat.

Jungle Beat

(Range of 5 Pitches)

© V. Johnson 1987

Let Everyone Move With Me

Age 3–7

Key Experiences

- Acting upon movement directions
- Moving in nonlocomotor ways
- Moving in locomotor ways
- Feeling and expressing steady beat
- Moving to music

Curriculum Concepts

Copying

Labels for movements

Children explore nonlocomotor and locomotor movement. One child is the leader, and all copy the leader's movement. Sing the song, matching the beat of the leader's movement.

Materials

Song: *Let Everyone Move With Me*

Activity to Experience

Help the children explore various ways to perform nonlocomotor and locomotor movements. Ask for several children to share their movements and all copy. Children are encouraged to talk about the movements.

One child volunteers to be the leader while the song is sung.

After the children begin to copy, add the **anchor word** if it is a steady beat movement, and then sing the song in the beat established. Substitute the child's name for "me" in the song. If the leader is doing a movement that has a label, or if the child suggests a label, use that in the song also. For example, "Let everyone swing arms like James."

Facilitation and Reflection

What would you call your movement?

How would you describe James's movement?

How is Tricia's movement different from James's movement?

What movements were easy to copy? Hard to copy?

Extensions

Children create a sequence by tapping two different parts of the body, one after the other, such as "KNEES, SHOULDERS." Substitute the name of the leader for "me" in the song. Each movement is performed on the macrobeat—two movements for each measure of music. In the first line of the song, tap the knees on "ev-'ry" and tap the shoulders on "move." Tap the knees again on "me" and the shoulders during the resting beat after the word "me."

If the children are school-aged, use different leaders—one right after the other. Signal each new child's turn by saying at the end of the song, "Show us your movement. You are next." After the child shows the movement begin the song again.

Let Everyone Move With Me

(Range of 8 Pitches)

Folk Song

* In this song, because of the slower tempo, the macrobeat appears as underlined.

Little Green Frog

Age 3–6

Key Experiences

- Moving in nonlocomotor ways
- Feeling and expressing steady beat
- Moving in sequences to a common beat
- Moving to music

Curriculum Concepts

Jumping up

Steady beat

Musical patterns

Children make their stuffed animals jump up. Wesley, who has the frog, decides where he wants to be kissed. He then begins the down/up movement, and the song is added.

Materials

One stuffed animal for each child

One little green frog

Song: *Little Green Frog*

Activity to Experience

Children are encouraged to make their animals jump up and to say the words "JUMP UP" with their motions.

Wesley has the frog and volunteers to be the leader. All copy his "jump up" movement. The teacher asks Wesley where he wants to be kissed at the end of the song. [He chooses his ear.] She speaks the **anchor words** JUMP UP to match Luis's timing and adds the song. At the end of the song the frog kisses Wesley on his ear and all make the kissing sound.

The **anchor pitch** can be used if the children are going to sing the song.

Other children volunteer to take the frog and be the leader. Christopher is next and will be kissed on his head.

Facilitation and Reflection

How do you show jumping up? Where do we have to start to jump up?

What other things besides our animal friends could jump up?

Extensions

All the animal friends can jump up. (Refer to the third verse of the song.)

The children can jump up.

Change the animal in the song, such as "Little Brown Bear."

Little Green Frog

(Range of 5 Pitches)

E. Carlton

One, two, sing with me.

1. Lit - tle green frog. Lit - tle green frog.
2. Lit - tle green frog. Lit - tle green frog.

Jump up! Jump up!
Jump up! Jump up!

Lit - tle green frog. Lit - tle green frog kiss
Lit - tle green frog. Lit - tle green frog kiss

Wes - ley on his ear. __
Chris-to - pher on the head. __

Verse 3: Animal friends. Animal friends.
Jump up! Jump up!
Animal friends. Animal friends, now
Kiss me on my chin.

Little Red Wagon

Age 3–6

Key Experiences

- Moving in nonlocomotor ways
- Expressing creativity

Curriculum Concepts

Moving body while sitting

Action words

Children are seated on a carpet square (their imaginary wagon). They suggest movements they could do while seated in the wagon. These movements are incorporated into the song.

Materials

One carpet square for each child

Song: *Little Red Wagon*

Activity to Experience

Each child is seated on a carpet square that represents his or her wagon. They explore movements they might do while seated in their wagon. The teacher sings the song while children do their movements.

Children share their ideas and the class copies.

One child is the leader, selecting a movement such as jiggle, and the class copies. The song is added, substituting jiggle, "Jiggle up and down in our little red wagon." The final line can add the leader's name: "We can jiggle with Eric."

Another child is the leader and all follow. *Note:* If the movement suggested can be put into a steady beat, such as "Waving to our friends," add the **anchor word** or **anchor pitch** before singing the song. The movement might be "rock" so the **anchor word** spoken 4 times is "ROCK, ROCK, ROCK, ROCK."

If the children have difficulty thinking of movements, suggest action words such as "shake," "thump," and "pound."

Facilitation and Reflection

How can we move our arms if we are sitting down? How can we move our legs?

What movements did you do on your carpet square, Patrick? Lucinda?

When different children were the leader, what movements did they do?

What is different about moving while sitting down and moving while standing up?

Extensions

School-aged children can work in pairs, or several children can occupy each wagon.

Children think of different colors for wagons and choose the movement and the wagon color when they are the leader.

Substitute other objects for the wagon, such as boats or cars.

Little Red Wagon

(Range of 8 Pitches)

Traditional Tune

1. We're all here in the lit-tle red wag-on.
2. Jig-gle up and down in the lit-tle red wag-on.

We're all here in the lit-tle red wag-on.
Jig-gle up and down in the lit-tle red wag-on.

We're all here in the lit-tle red wag-on.
Jig-gle up and down in the lit-tle red wag-on.

Won't you be my good friend?
Won't you be my good friend?

Verse 3: Wavin' to our friends in the little red wagon.
Wavin' to our friends in the little red wagon.
Wavin' to our friends in the little red wagon.
Won't you be my good friend?

(Children may share ideas for other verses.)

Making Cookies
(The Muffin Man)

Age 3–7

Key Experiences

- Moving in nonlocomotor ways
- Expressing creativity
- Moving to music

Curriculum Concepts

Representation

Shapes

Roll, stir, cut

Children have already made cookies before beginning this action song. In this activity, they represent the various actions they used in making the cookies.

Materials

One carpet square per child, if needed

Song: *Making Cookies*

Activity to Experience

The adult might begin by engaging the children in a recall of how they made the cookies the day before. The children recall the ingredients they used and all the things they had to do to get the cookies ready to bake and then to eat.

Have the children keep steady beat while the adult sings the first verse of the song.

Then ask the children what they did first when they made cookies. Jeffrey said they had to stir the cookie dough after all the ingredients were in the bowl. Everyone is encouraged to pretend to stir the cookie dough while the second verse is sung.

Anna says they rolled out the cookie dough next. The teacher sings the third verse while they imitate the action of rolling out the dough on their carpet square.

Steven adds that they cut the cookie shapes on the dough, so the children pretend to cut the shapes with their imaginary cookie cutters. Verse 4 is added.

Next, the children pretend to put the cookies in the oven and then to smell the cookies while they bake. Verses 5 and 6 are sung.

Children finally pretend to eat the cookies.

Sing the song again and see how many of the children can join in singing while the actions are represented again. Begin with the **anchor pitch.**

Facilitation and Reflection

How would you make with your bodies one of the shapes that the cookie cutters made?

What did we do next (referring to the order of the steps in making and baking the cookies)?

How did you stir the cookie dough? Roll out the cookie dough?

Extensions

Represent other sequenced activities, such as a trip to the apple orchard or a trip to the fire station.

Making Cookies

(Range of 6 Pitches)

Traditional Tune

Verse 2: We will stir our cookie dough . . .
and then we'll roll it out.
Verse 3: We'll roll out the cookie dough . . .
and then we'll cut the shapes.
Verse 4: We will cut a cookie shape . . .
and put it on the pan.
Verse 5: The oven's ready, put them in . . .
set the timer on.
Verse 6: Smell the cookies while they bake . . .
I can hardly wait.
Verse 7: Eat the cookies while they're warm . . .
Yum, yum, good!

Old King Glory
(Modified version of this singing game)

Age 4–7

Key Experiences

- Moving in nonlocomotor ways
- Moving in locomotor ways
- Feeling and expressing steady beat
- Moving to music

Curriculum Concepts

Steady beat

The concept of "around"

Traveling outside of a circle

Children find ways to keep steady beat. A child leader in the center of the circle chooses a way to keep steady beat that all copy. Another child (the King or Queen) makes a plan for traveling around outside the circle.

Materials

Crown for the King or Queen

Song: *Old King Glory*

Activity to Experience

The adult leads a steady beat movement using both hands against the body, such as patting on the head. Children are encouraged to explore other places to keep steady beat.

The child who volunteers to be the leader goes to the center of the circle and chooses a steady beat movement, and the others copy.

Another child volunteers to be King or Queen Glory. That child makes a plan for how to travel around the outside of the circle. The volunteer travels while the others keep steady beat and the song is sung. You could substitute the name of the child for "Glory."

The singing game continues with two different children volunteering for the two parts.

Facilitation and Reflection

How do you know that you are keeping the beat steady?

What way did you choose to keep steady beat? (Ask several children.)

How are you going to travel around the outside of the circle, Zubin?

How did you know what child would follow the leader around the circle?

Extensions

Kindergarten and older children may enjoy a more complicated version of this singing game. On the words "first one, second one, third follow me" the child traveling taps three children in sequence. The third one tapped (or all three tapped) follows the child traveling and copies the traveling movement.

You might wish to have the leader in the center of the circle wear something special, such as a cape, and the King or Queen wear a crown.

Old King Glory

(Range of 8 Pitches)

Traditional Tune

One, two, sing with me.

Old King Glo - ry of the moun - tain. The

moun - tain was so high, it near - ly touched the sky. The

first one, the sec - ond one, the third fol - low me.

Old Man Mosie

Age 5-7

Key Experiences

- Acting upon movement directions
- Moving in nonlocomotor ways
- Moving in locomotor ways
- Expressing creativity
- Moving in sequences to a common beat

Curriculum Concepts

Older vs. younger

Sick vs. well

Turning around

Going away

Children listen to the song as the adult sings it. They talk about things that happen in the song. The various movements contained in the action song are sequenced and then performed.

Materials

A long stick or cane for each child (optional)

Song: *Old Man Mosie*

Activity to Experience

Children are seated. The adult sings the song, and the children listen for things that happen in the song. They discuss the things that happened.

Children are asked about characteristics of older and younger people. They are asked if they have seen an older person use a cane. Debra volunteers to show how her grandfather uses a cane. All the children try walking with their "canes."

Children talk about differences of being well and being sick. They represent an adult calling the doctor.

The first part of the song is sung, pausing after each phrase, and the children act out walking with a cane and calling the doctor.

Before the middle part of the song is sung, children try stepping forward and turning around. The first three lines (phrases) of the song are sung, and the children sequence the actions.

If the children are familiar with the *Hokey Pokey,* they can use the sequences in that song to plan a way to "get out of town." The adult says, "I will count to 8 while you show how you will leave to 'get out of town.'"

The song is sung in its entirety and all do the actions.

The song then is repeated when another doctor is called.

Facilitation and Reflection

How would you describe the difference between older and younger people?

What is the difference between when you are sick and when you are well?

What are different ways you can call the doctor?

How did you leave town or "get out of town"?

Extensions

A child leader decides to be old or young and changes the words of the song, such as "Young boy Kevin sick in the head" or "Old lady Kristin . . ."

Children represent old in any way they wish—not necessarily by using a cane.

Change "Do the Hokey Pokey" to the child's idea, such as "Skip in a circle."

Old Man Mosie

(Range of 6 Pitches)

Traditional Tune

One In a Boat
(Two In a Boat)

Age 4–7

Key Experiences

- ○━ Moving in nonlocomotor ways
- ○━ Feeling and expressing steady beat
- ○━ Moving in sequences to a common beat
- ○━ Moving to music

Curriculum Concepts

Bend and straighten

Rocking

Children represent a motion of rowing a boat. As they bend and straighten their arms, they rock forward and backward. The song is added.

Materials

Song: *One In a Boat*

Activity to Experience

Ask the children if they have ever been in a rowboat. Have the children rock back and forth as you sing the song. *Note:* The words or syllables underlined represent the macrobeat (rocking beat).

Discuss rowing a boat. Demonstrate a straightening and bending motion that the children copy. Add the song to the established timing.

Suggest to the children that they rock forward and backward while they straighten and bend their arms. After they try this out, one child is the leader and all copy. The **anchor word** or **anchor pitch** is added, and the two verses of the song are sung.

When the children are successful, have 5–7-year-olds try rocking in pairs. Let them solve the problem of how they will rock together. One pair demonstrates their way of rocking, and all the pairs copy. The **anchor word** or **anchor pitch** then is added and the song is sung, "Two In a Boat."

Facilitation and Reflection

To those of you who have been in a rowboat, what did the person rowing have to do to make the boat move?

How can we straighten and bend our arms to show rowing?

What different ways can we rock when we are sitting down?

When you had a partner, how did you decide to work together to row your boat?

Extensions

Suggest that more than one or two children go in a boat and let them decide how they want to row the boat. If they sit one behind the other, each person could represent rowing with two oars. If children sit side by side in pairs, they each could represent rowing with one oar.

For children in grade 2 and older: Have them decide how they would make the boat go in the other direction.

One In a Boat

(Range of 8 Pitches)

Adapted Traditional Tune

One, two, sing with me!

1. One in a boat and the tide rolls high.
2. Rockin' in a boat and the tide rolls high.

One in a boat and the tide rolls high.
Rockin' in a boat and the tide rolls high.

One in a boat and the tide rolls high.
Rockin' in a boat and the tide rolls high.

Get you a pret-ty one bye and bye.
See me rock my boat as I rock bye 'n bye.

Get you a pret-ty one bye and bye.
See me rock my boat as I rock bye 'n bye.

Pizza Hut
(A Ram Sam Sam)

Age 3-7

Key Experiences

○━ Moving in nonlocomotor ways

○━ Feeling and expressing steady beat

○━ Moving in sequences to a common beat

○━ Moving to music

Curriculum Concepts

Representation

Moving and speaking

ABA form

Children copy the movements of the adult and make suggestions about each movement and what it represents. The first two movements are sequenced and the words for the song are spoken. The same procedure follows through the other sections of the song.

Materials

Song: *Pizza Hut*

Activity to Experience

The adult demonstrates the first movement of making a circle in front of the body with the fingertips touching (pizza shape). The children copy and suggest what the shape might represent.

The adult now puts both arms overhead with the palms of the hands together (in the shape of the hut). This second movement is added, and the children copy and suggest what the shape represents.

The words "Pizza Hut" are added to the movements. All speak the words and do the movements simultaneously.

The teacher flaps her arms against her body (like a chicken) and children copy and suggest what the movement represents. Do two flaps while speaking "Kentucky Fried Chicken." Try it several times. The sequence for "Pizza Hut" follows one time.

Put the entire verse together with the words.

Now add the movement to represent McDonald's. Raise the pointer fingers straight up and around to simulate the McDonald's "golden arches." The children copy and describe. Add the words.

Do the entire sequence with the words; then add the song while the children do the movements.

Facilitation and Reflection

What might this circle shape be? (Ask for the other shapes also.)

How do we know when to speak the words?

What other fast food restaurants in our town could we represent with movement (Burger King, Dairy Queen, etc.)?

Extensions

Sing the song first and have the children think of ways to represent the various places mentioned. Then use the children's ideas for the song.

Children might think of other places that could be substituted in the song, such as Burger King, Dairy Queen, Taco Bell, etc., and then plan movements that could represent those places.

For students aged 7 and older: Add the second verse of the song and suggest that the students do the movements—8 marching steps, 2 jumps, 4 marching steps; 4 skating steps (macrobeat tempo), 2 jumps, 4 marching steps. Suggest that the students add other locomotor or nonlocomotor movements to the song.

Extensions into other curricular areas where movement naturally reinforces specific words include these concepts:

Adding:
   2 plus 2 (sung 3 times), and the sum is 4.

Opposites:
   up and down (2 times), up and down are opposites.

Rhyming words:
   hat and cat (2 times), hat and cat are rhyming words.

Fruits:
   cantaloupe (2 times), tiny grapes and a cantaloupe...

Pizza Hut

(Range of 5 Pitches)

Gift to Phyllis S. Weikart from
Sydney, Australia, Music Educators

One, two, read-y, sing.

1. Piz - za Hut! Piz - za Hut! Ken - tuck - y Fried Chick - en and a Piz - za Hut!
2. March in place. March in place. Jump two times and you march in place.

Piz - za Hut! Piz - za Hut! Ken - tuck - y Fried Chick -en and a Piz - za Hut! Mc -
March in place. March in place. Jump two times and you march in place. Go

Don - ald's, Mc - Don - ald's, Ken - tuck - y Fried Chick - en and a Piz - za Hut! Mc -
skat - ing, go skat - ing. Jump two times and you march in place. Go

Don - ald's, Mc - Don - ald's, Ken - tuck - y Fried Chick - en and a Piz - za Hut!
skat - ing, go skat - ing. Jump two times and you march in place.

Piz - za Hut! Piz - za Hut! Ken - tuck - y Fried Chick - en and a Piz - za Hut!
March in place. March in place. Jump two times and you march in place.

Piz - za Hut! Piz - za Hut! Ken - tuck - y Fried Chick - en and a Piz - za Hut!
March in place. March in place. Jump two times and you march in place.

Rock-a-Bye, Baby

Age 3–6

Key Experiences

- Moving in nonlocomotor ways
- Feeling and expressing steady beat
- Moving to music
- Singing songs

Curriculum Concepts

Rocking

Moving and singing

Children find different ways to rock. The song is added to the rocking beat.

Materials

Stuffed animal or a doll (optional)

Song: *Rock-a-Bye, Baby*

Activity to Experience

Children are seated in a random formation. They explore rocking and talk about the different ways they are rocking.

One child is the leader and the others copy. The adult adds the **anchor word** "ROCK" spoken 4 times, matching the leader's tempo, and adds the song. *Note:* The underlined words or syllables should match the rocking beat. When the children are ready to join in singing the song, substitute the **anchor pitch** to set the beat and first pitch of the song.

Repeat with other children as leaders. You may wish to substitute the leader's name for the word "baby."

Facilitation and Reflection

What does it mean to rock?

What different ways did you find to rock?

How is Jose's way of rocking the same or different than Suzie's?

Who was rocking fast? Who was rocking in a slower way?

Extensions

Each child holds and rocks a stuffed animal or doll. The adult might hold one child while the others rock their animals or dolls.

Older children may enjoy rocking together with a partner. Suggest that two children both sit inside a Hula-Hoop or both hold the hoop and find a way to rock together.

Have all of the children gather in a circle or in a line and then rock together.

Rock-a-Bye, Baby

(Range of 9 Pitches)

Traditional Tune

One, two, read-y, sing.

Rock - a- bye, ba - by, on the tree - top.

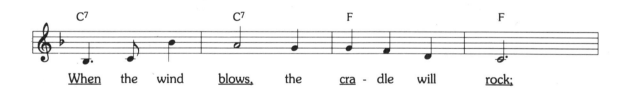

When the wind blows, the cra - dle will rock;

when the birds sing, the ba - by will smile, and

fall a- sleep hap - py in a short while.

Shake Our Bells
(Jingle Bells)

Age 3–7

Key Experiences

- Moving with objects
- Expressing creativity
- Moving to music
- Exploring and identifying sounds

Curriculum Concepts

Shaking

Moving and singing

Children have one or two bells they shake while the song is sung.

Materials

One or two bells for each child

Song: *Shake Our Bells*

Activity to Experience

Begin by suggesting that children explore a bell-ringing (shaking) motion with each hand if they have only one bell. You might say to the children who are using one hand with one bell, "Try shaking the bell with the other hand." If the children in your class each have two bells, have them shake with one bell in each hand.

Brian volunteers to be the leader and to show everyone a way to shake the bell(s) during the song. Use Brian's name in the song.

Suggest that children find different places to shake the bells, such as up high, down low, to one side, etc.

Facilitation and Reflection

Where did you shake your bell—in front of you, up high, down low?

Did the leaders shake their bells in a fast or in a slow way?

Where is Leigh showing us to shake our bells?

Extensions

Substitute rhythm sticks and discover different ways to make sounds with them. Change the song as follows: "Make a sound, Make a sound, Make a sound like_____."

Use the song on other special days, such as Valentine's Day. Each child has a heart cut out of paper. They pat the beat on their heart. The song might be,

"*Beating hearts, beating hearts, beating steadily.*

Pat the beat upon your heart, this is Valentine's Day."

Shake Our Bells

(Range of 5 Pitches)

Traditional Tune

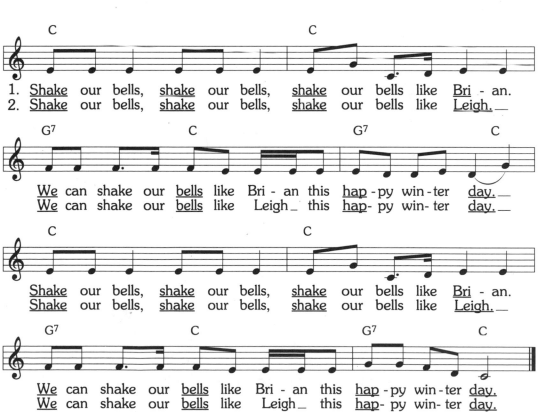

Shape Song
(Here We Go Round the Mulberry Bush)

Age 3–7

Key Experiences

- Acting upon movement directions
- Moving in nonlocomotor ways
- Moving to music

Curriculum Concepts

Shapes

Statues

Children make statue shapes that are copied by the other children. Sing the song with the leader's name in it.

Materials

One carpet square or Hula-Hoop for each child

Song: *Shape Song*

Activity to Experience

The adult begins by making a statue shape that the children copy. Facilitate their awareness with appropriate questions. Add the song with the adult's name (Cathy) used in the song.

Ask if a child will volunteer to make the next statue shape while the song is song. Bradley wants to be the leader. He makes a shape while the song is sung. At the end of the song encourage the children to make the same statue shape. Again ask questions about the shape.

Facilitation and Reflection

Look at the arms. Where are they—up high or down low?

Look at the feet. What do you see?

Look at the head. What do you see?

What do you notice about Bradley's statue shape? Samantha's shape?

Extensions

School-aged children could make partner statues.

The statue shape could be made with one part of the body moving, such as the wrist bending and straightening to the beat of the song.

Suggest that a child specify a position for everyone's statue, such as standing, lying down, or sitting.

Shape Song

(Range of 8 Pitches)

Traditional Tune

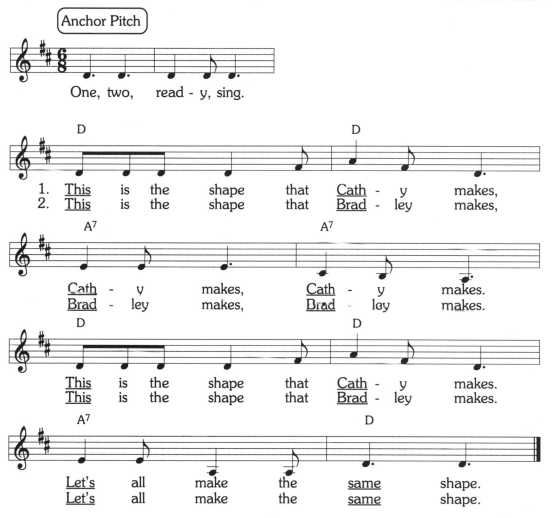

One, two, read - y, sing.

1. This is the shape that Cath - y makes,
2. This is the shape that Brad - ley makes,

Cath - y makes, Cath - y makes.
Brad - ley makes, Brad - ley makes.

This is the shape that Cath - y makes.
This is the shape that Brad - ley makes.

Let's all make the same shape.
Let's all make the same shape.

Someone Is the Leader

Age 3–7

Key Experiences
- Moving in nonlocomotor ways
- Moving in locomotor ways
- Feeling and expressing steady beat
- Moving to music
- Singing songs

Curriculum Concepts
Copying

Steady beat

Children copy the leader's steady beat movement. The song is added to the beat established by the leader.

Materials
Song: *Someone Is the Leader*

Activity to Experience
Children are encouraged to explore steady beat movements with their hands and arms and with their legs and feet. The children are asked to describe their steady beat movements and how they know they are keeping steady beat.

Cindy volunteers to be the leader in the center of the circle. She has planned a marching movement. The other children copy Cindy. The adult speaks the **anchor word** "MARCH" 8 times to Cindy's beat and then sings the song.

The activity continues with another child as the leader.

When the children are ready to add the song, the **anchor pitch** precedes the singing of the song to establish the steady beat and beginning pitch of the song.

Facilitation and Reflection
Describe your steady beat movement. How did you know you were keeping it steady?

What was Cindy's steady beat movement?

What did you have to do to copy Cindy's marching movement?

Extensions

Encourage the child in the center to set a steady beat movement, which the children copy. At the end of the song, the leader makes a statue shape and everyone copies. Change the second line of the song to "She will make a statue shape, and we will do the same."

The leader makes a plan for how he will travel around the room at the end of the song. He shares his plan with the teacher. Before the song is sung, the leader sets a steady beat, the **anchor word** or **anchor pitch** is added, and the song sung. The last line of the song becomes: *"He will jump around the room, and we will do the same."*

Someone Is the Leader

(Range of 6 Pitches)

Melody by Marcelyn Smale

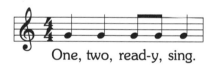

One, two, read-y, sing.

1. Some - one is the lead - er, Cin - dy is her name.
2. Some - one is the lead - er, Ste - ven is his name.

Ev - 'ry - thing that she does, we will do the same.
Ev - 'ry - thing that he does, we will do the same.

Start Your Day

Age 3–6

Key Experiences

- Moving in nonlocomotor ways
- Moving in sequences to a common beat
- Moving to music
- Singing songs

Curriculum Concepts

The concept of "up"

Waving

Cheering

Children listen to the song and suggest ways to do the movements mentioned in the song. They sequence the movements and add them to the song.

Materials

Song: *Start Your Day*

Activity to Experience

Children listen to the song as it is sung by the adult and suggest words in the song that could be shown with movement—hug, smile, give the "thumbs up" sign, wave to friends, give a cheer.

Children are encouraged to suggest ways to do the movements. All agree on the way to hug and do the other movements.

The song is sung and the adult pauses at the end of each set of directions to give children time to do the movements.

Once the song is familiar, children sing or chime in where they can. If several children are singing from the beginning, the adult sings the **anchor pitch** to bring them in on the first pitch of the song.

Facilitation and Reflection

Who has a suggestion as to how we could hug?

What does it mean to put our thumbs up? Are there other parts of the body, such as our hands, that can show the idea of "up"?

How are we going to wave? What does waving mean?

How are we going to give a cheer? What are other ways to cheer?

Extensions

Encourage the children to think of other ways to start and end the day that would be different than giving a hug. Other words or concepts could also be changed.

Encourage the children to rock as the song is sung. Older children might wish to skate to the macrobeat (represented by the underlined words in the song).

Start Your Day

(Range of 6 Pitches)

E. Carlton

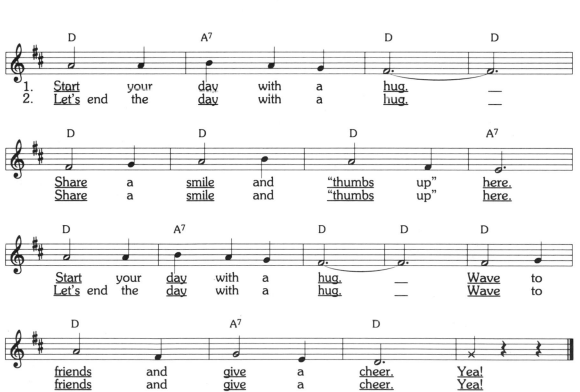

Statue Shapes

Age 4-7

Key Experiences

- Acting upon movement directions
- Moving in nonlocomotor ways
- Moving in locomotor ways
- Expressing creativity
- Moving to music

Curriculum Concepts

Statue shapes

The concept of "change"

Steady beat

Children have made several statue shapes and explored keeping some part of the statue in steady beat. Children now respond to the song's directions.

Materials

Song: *Statue Shapes*

Activity to Experience

Children explore making statue shapes.

They discuss what it means to make a change in their statue shape. They explore changing their statue shapes.

Children copy the adult's statue with a steady beat movement. They try a steady beat movement with their statue. They also explore moving their statue shape around the space.

The children each make a statue shape, and the adult sings the four verses of the song.

Facilitation and Reflection

Why do we call your shapes "statue shapes"?

What does it mean to change something? How did you change your statue shape?

How did you keep steady beat in your statue shape?

Why is it hard to move around in a statue shape?

Extensions

One child makes a shape, and the other children copy the shape. The leader also changes the statue, puts a part of the statue in steady beat, and moves around according to the words in the other verses of the songs.

School-aged children can work in pairs; one makes a statue, and the other copies for the parts of the song. The partner of the statue maker makes the changes, puts a part in steady beat, and helps the statue move around.

Statue Shapes

(Range of 9 Pitches)

Children's Play Song

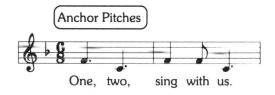

One, two, sing with us.

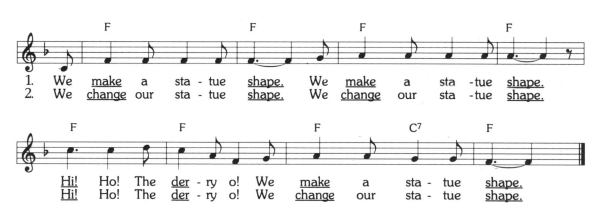

1. We make a sta-tue shape. We make a sta-tue shape.
2. We change our sta-tue shape. We change our sta-tue shape.

Hi! Ho! The der-ry o! We make a sta-tue shape.
Hi! Ho! The der-ry o! We change our sta-tue shape.

Verse 3: Our statues move in beat.
Our statues move in beat.
Hi! Ho! The derry-o!
Our statues move in beat.

Verse 4: Our statues move around.
Our statues move around.
Hi! Ho! The derry-o!
Our statues move around.

Teddy Bear

Age 3–6

Key Experiences

- Moving in nonlocomotor ways
- Expressing creativity
- Feeling and expressing steady beat
- Moving to music

Curriculum Concepts

Patting motions

Learner SAY & DO

The concepts of "slow" and "fast"

Each child holds a teddy bear. Children have their teddy bears pat steady beat on various parts of their bodies. They chant the name of the part using Learner SAY & DO and then respond as the song is sung.

Materials

A teddy bear for each child

Song: *Teddy Bear*

Activity to Experience

Suggest that the children explore ways that they can make their teddy bears pat various parts of their bodies, or the children can walk the feet of their teddy bears.

One child volunteers to be the leader and to choose a part of the body for all the teddy bears to pat.

The children practice the patting motion with Learner SAY & DO. For example they might make the bears pat their knees and chant "KNEES, KNEES, KNEES, KNEES" as the bears pat.

The child leader begins the patting movement, all copy while the **anchor word** is spoken, and the song is added. The beat of the song should match the beat the children have established.

If the walking movement is selected, SAY & DO "WALK, WALK, WALK, WALK." Change the song to "Teddy Bear, Teddy Bear walks his feet."

If the children are going to sing, begin with the **anchor pitch.**

Facilitation and Reflection

Where were your teddy bears patting?

How did you know when to say the word "KNEES"?

When you walked the teddy bear's feet, was it faster or slower than patting?

What does it mean to go slower? Faster?

Extensions

Substitute baby dolls or the child's favorite stuffed animal and change the words of the song to fit, such as "Animal Friends, Animal Friends . . ."

Children might show static movements with their animals that the other children copy.

Teddy Bear

(Range of 5 Pitches)

Afro-American Folk Song

One, two, sing with me.

C

1. Ted - dy Bear, Ted - dy Bear pats his knees. ___
2. Ted - dy Bear, Ted - dy Bear pats his nose. ___

G⁷

Ted - dy Bear, Ted - dy Bear pats his knees. ___
Ted - dy Bear, Ted - dy Bear pats his nose. ___

C

Ted - dy Bear, Ted - dy Bear pats his knees. ___
Ted - dy Bear, Ted - dy Bear pats his nose. ___

G⁷ **C**

Ted - dy Bear, Ted - dy Bear hug me please.
Ted - dy Bear, Ted - dy Bear hug me close!

Two Little Red Birds

Age 4–7

Key Experiences

- Moving in nonlocomotor ways
- Moving in locomotor ways
- Expressing creativity
- Moving to music
- Exploring the singing voice

Curriculum Concepts

"Flying away"

"Coming back"

Vocal exploration

Children pretend to fly while sitting on their "wall." They "fly away" around the room. They come back to their own "wall."

Materials

One carpet square and one large block for each child

Song: *Two Little Red Birds*

Activity to Experience

A block is placed on each carpet square, which serves as the "tree." Each child finds a "tree" to sit in.

The children move their arms to represent flying and use vocal exploration with their flying. They talk about how they are flying and what their voices are doing.

Now half of the group moves about the space as if the children are "flying away," being careful not to bump into each other. This group represents "Elizabeth" in the song. The other half, representing "Brie," does the same. Only half of the group is moving at a time.

They "come back" to their "trees." The Elizabeth group comes back first.

The song is sung, and the children respond when it is their group's time to "fly away" and to "come back."

The second verse of the song is added, substituting seagulls and the boys' names (Bob and Dave).

Facilitation and Reflection

How did you fly when you were sitting in your tree?

How did you "fly away" when it was your turn? How did you keep from bumping others?

What else flies away besides birds?

What did you do on the words "come back"?

Extensions

Two girls volunteer to become "Elizabeth" and "Brie," and their names are substituted in the song.

Two boys volunteer for the second verse.

You might look at the children's clothing colors and call them bluebirds or yellow birds.

Two Little Red Birds

(Range of 6 Pitches)

Traditional Tune

* Vocal improvisation: 1. low to high
                                  2. high to low

Where Is Thumbkin?

Age 3–7

Key Experiences

- Moving in nonlocomotor ways
- Moving in sequences to a common beat
- Moving to music

Curriculum Concepts

Alternating movement

Conversations

Children follow the adult's demonstration and verbal directions for this action song.

Materials

Song: *Where Is Thumbkin?*

Activity to Experience

Demonstrate putting both hands behind your back, and encourage the children to copy. Then bring both hands in front at the same time and have the children copy. Put them behind your back again and this time bring them in front with thumbs up. Ask the children about the difference in the movement this time. Next demonstrate putting one hand at a time in front with the thumb up, while the children notice the difference.

Sing the first two lines of the song. The hands are behind the back for line 1; the thumbs come out one at a time for line 2.

Next ask the children how they would make the thumbs talk to each other. If necessary demonstrate one thumb wiggling and then the other thumb wiggling.

Add the third line of the song to lines 1 and 2.

Ask the children what they would do to have one thumb run away and then the other thumb run away. Let one child choose the way and all copy.

Now sing the entire song and have the children do the movements.

Facilitation and Reflection

What did I do differently the second time I brought my hands out? What did I do the next time?

What are your thumbs saying to one another? Did one thumb talk and then the other one?

Where did they go when they ran away?

Extensions

Have the children do the song with the other fingers, such as "Where is ring man?"

Try it with the feet as children are seated: "Where is big foot? Where is big foot?"

Try it with children's names. For example, sing "Where is Kevin?" and have Kevin's thumbs talk to each other.

Where Is Thumbkin?

(Range of 9 Pitches)

Traditional Tune

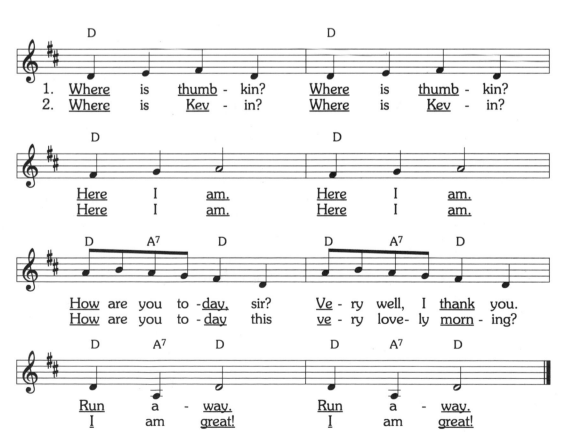

1. Where is thumb - kin? Where is thumb - kin?
2. Where is Kev - in? Where is Kev - in?

Here I am. Here I am.
Here I am. Here I am.

How are you to - day, sir? Ve - ry well, I thank you.
How are you to - day this ve - ry love- ly morn - ing?

Run a - way. Run a - way.
I am great! I am great!

Winter Time Is Here
(Jimmy Crack Corn)

Age 3–7

Key Experiences

- Moving in nonlocomotor ways
- Feeling and expressing steady beat
- Moving to music

Curriculum Concepts

Steady beat

Shaking

Same and different

Children explore shaking the bells in various places. When children are the leaders, sing the song with their movements added.

Materials

Two sleigh bells for each child

Song: *Winter Time Is Here*

Activity to Experience

Children explore shaking their bells in various places around their bodies. Note that the bells are held with one in each hand. Hands (or other body parts) can be substituted if you do not have bells.

The adult shakes her bells in front of her and says, "I'm shaking my bells in front of me. Who found another place to shake the bells?" Children are encouraged to talk about where they are shaking their bells.

When the children seem comfortable, ask "Who is shaking the bells up high?" Have a child who answers become the leader and all copy. Add the song. Have another child using a different location be the leader, all copy, and add the song substituting the new location.

Facilitation and Reflection

Where were you shaking your bells? Is your place the same as Maria's place?

What kind of sounds do the bells make?

Where were some of the places we used to shake the bells to the song?

Extensions

Do other movements without the bells, and adapt the song accordingly. One example might be "Twist both arms in front of you (sung three times), as we keep the beat."

Do locomotor movement with the song, such as "March your feet around the room (sung three times), keep the microbeat."

Winter Time Is Here

(Range of 9 Pitches)

Traditional Tune

One, two, read-y, sing!

D / A⁷
* Shake those bells __ and shake them high. __

A⁷ / D
Shake those bells __ and shake them high. __

D / G
Shake those bells __ and shake them high, __ for

A⁷ / D
win - ter time is here. __ __ __

* Children naturally play bells on the microbeat, as indicated by the underlines.

Zach Pats His Knees
(Jimmy Crack Corn)

Age 3–7

Key Experiences

- Moving in nonlocomotor ways
- Feeling and expressing steady beat
- Moving to music

Curriculum Concepts

Patting

Body part identification

Children are encouraged to pat steady beat on different parts of their bodies. One child is the leader, and the song is sung.

Materials

Song: *Zach Pats His Knees*

Activity to Experience

The adult initiates patting her chin with both hands and encourages the children to join her. She tells the children that she is patting steady beat.

The adult suggests that the children find other places to pat steady beat and to share their beat-keeping.

Zach volunteers to keep steady beat on his knees. When all are copying, the adults speaks the **anchor word** "KNEES" 4 times and adds the song.

As other children become the leader, their names are substituted in the song.

If the children are going to try to sing, the adult uses the **anchor pitch** to bring all into steady beat and supply the first notes of the song.

Facilitation and Reflection

What different parts of the body did we pat in steady beat?

What does it mean to pat?

How did we know the beat the steady?

Extensions

All pat their head and sing the second verse of the song.

Substitute walking to the steady beat and sing "We walk our feet and keep the beat."

Substitute other movements and change the song to fit the movements.

Zach Pats His Knees

(Range of 9 Pitches)

Traditional Tune

One, two, sing with us!

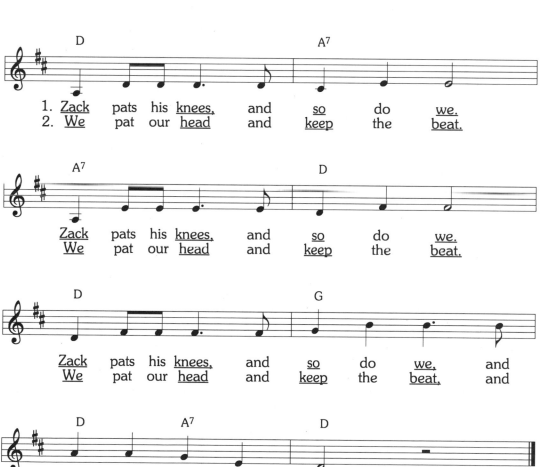

1. Zack pats his knees, and so do we.
2. We pat our head and keep the beat.

Zack pats his knees, and so do we.
We pat our head and keep the beat.

Zack pats his knees, and so do we, and
We pat our head and keep the beat, and

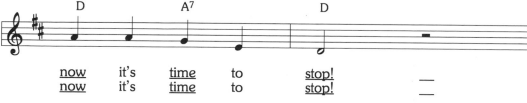

now it's time to stop! __
now it's time to stop! __

About the Author

Phyllis S. Weikart, Director of the program "Education Through Movement: Building the Foundation," is one of the country's leading authorities on movement-based active learning. She bases her approach to teaching on her ongoing work with students of all ages—from preschoolers to senior citizens. She is the author of numerous movement and dance books, including *Foundations in Elementary Education: Movement; Round the Circle: Key Experiences in Movement for Children; Movement Plus Music: Activities for Children Ages 3 to 7; Movement in Steady Beat;* and *Teaching Folk Dance: Successful Steps.* She is the co-author of *Foundations in Elementary Education: Music,* with Elizabeth B. Carlton, and co-author of *Cultures and Styling in Folk Dance,* with Sanna Longden. In addition, she developed the *Rhythmically Moving 1–9* and *Changing Directions 1–6* musical recording series, and the *Beginning Folk Dances Illustrated 1–6* demonstration videos.

Associate Professor Emeritus in the Division of Kinesiology, University of Michigan, and visiting Associate Professor at Hartt School of Music, Weikart is also Movement Consultant for the High/Scope Educational Research Foundation. Her formal education includes a B.S. degree from Beaver College in Pennsylvania and an M.A. degree from the University of Michigan. In addition to being a nationally known and highly respected educator-author, Weikart is a researcher, curriculum developer, workshop leader, choreographer, and promoter of high-quality international folk dance recordings. Through her wide-ranging experiences, Phyllis S. Weikart has developed an approach to teaching that ensures the success of both teachers and students.